www.tredition.de

AF206941

www.tredition.de

© 2018 Susan Princess Reuss
www.susanreuss.de

Publisher: tredition GmbH, Hamburg

ISBN
Paperback: 978-3-7439-5465-6
Hardcover: 978-3-7439-5466-3
e-Book: 978-3-7439-5467-0

Photo credits: private, © fotolia.com

Susan Princess Reuss

Persia, my home

*I dedicate this narration to my Homeland Iran and its incredible people,
to whom I owe many unforgettable moments.*

*We are all citizens of one world, but in our souls we reserve a special
place for our own ancestral land in which we were born and took roots,
where we learned how to love and to be loved, how to forgive and forget,
where we share the same destiny, where we learned the sacred meaning
of being one with others, the meaning of family.*

*Persia, with her ancient and majestic history, culture, globally
renowned for exquisite poetry and philosophy stood proud and brave
since the dawn of history for justice, equality and tolerance. She
endured brutal foreign invasions and occupations, but through all that,
remained true to the core of Persian values:
good words, good deeds, and good thoughts.
She enriched, enchanted and shaped me forever.*

Contents

Arriving

On a flight to my homeland, I close my eyes, immersed in thought, and let my mind take me on a journey down memory lane. The memories of my childhood home are still alive and ingrained in the innermost layer of my soul. I can smell the aroma of those still and quiet days even as I am flown through the air at 35,000 feet. I can feel Tehran in my soul.

Today, Iranians are scattered all over the world. They are everywhere, and yet nowhere at the same time. No matter where they may go, they generally will never feel at home. Maybe that's why they often feel lonely regardless of where they reside, especially if separated from families and loved ones. The younger generation lives their lives overseas in solitude, while their parents are rotting in loneliness until death in the homeland. Often, financial constraints and political conflicts get in the way of children returning from overseas to attend their parents' funerals or to say a last goodbye. As a result, children and parents both tend to feel forgotten whether they are overseas or left behind. We, the Persians overseas, feel forgotten by our families, our friends and our classmates. And we forget about them, too.

For those who leave the homeland, survival takes over, demanding that feelings of loneliness, connections, even love, are suppressed. The past must stay in the past for those who need to keep moving forward to survive. There is no other way.

On the plane, a fervent and friendly atmosphere is permeating the air. The passengers are smiling, greeting each other, exchanging their seats and even taking care of other passengers' children. I feel relieved. After four and a half hours, I arrive in Teheran.

Do and Don't –

Tips for Iran travelers

During developments in recent years, Iran increasingly draws interest from tourists and business people. But everyone looking to travel to Iran must be aware that there are certain rules in place that must be abided by.

Clothes: According to the rules of Islam, women are required to wear a scarf and their clothes can't fit too tightly. Also, clothes must cover everything up to the ankles and wrists. Men should abstain from wearing shorts.

Customs Regulations: It is forbidden to bring alcohol, pork and magazines or books containing explicit images into the country.

Money: Paying with credit cards is rarely possible and it's usually impossible to withdraw cash with foreign bank cards. The national currency Rial can be obtained in exchange offices or by exchanging at banks.

Religion: The rules of Islam generally must be obeyed by non-Muslims as well. For example, it is not allowed to smoke, drink or eat in public during Ramadan.

Safety: Those wishing to explore Iran outside of Tehran should contact their home country's embassy to learn about risks and travel advice. At this time, travel to areas near the borders of Turkey, Iraq, Pakistan and Afghanistan is discouraged.

City of Tehran

Tehran is a frantic city. It is crazy, limitless, sprawling, loud, stinky and dirty. At the same time, it is a vivid, exuberant and inimitably beautiful place. It radiates an abundance of positive energy and charisma. Tehran has recovered from the melancholy and violent experiences of its past. However, despite all the calamities and economic hardships it's endured, the people of Tehran have remained amicable and friendly; they have successfully sustained a positive aura in the city.

The people who live in Tehran are the embodiment of its character. They believe in the power of faith and forgiveness, and have learned how to endure the unendurable with a smile.

Tehranis are humorous and are always in a good mood. They are talkative and have a zest for life. Even when spending a short amount of time in stores, busses or restaurants, they like to tell jokes and have a good time. Subjects pertaining to air pollution, contaminated water, junk food, traffic jams, noise pollution, overpriced commodities, and a lack of pharmaceuticals or medical care are all addressed humbly with a benign smile.

Despite their humor though, Iranians are typically not good listeners. They don't want to contemplate or worry about things. The song "Don't worry, be happy "is a perfect representation of their attitude towards life. They only want to live and breathe freely; all the while being left alone.

Nowadays, Iranians like to distract themselves with Turkish or Indian movies, as there are restrictions on Persian movies that prohibit their casts from being able to act freely, dance, sing, embrace each other, or do anything that young people may potentially interpret as romance. Since the actresses must wear scarves and long coats, people prefer movies and TV shows from Turkey or India to distract them from their daily lives. Iranians love beautiful clothes, fashion, color, style and good-looking actors, and unfortunately, glamour has been taken away from their movies. Iranians only desire to indulge themselves in what is beautiful. This admiration for beauty is perhaps traced back to the history of their great Persian Empire.

After many years of enduring suffering, sorrows, war, sanctions, and political uproar that made them exhausted and worn out, they are now seeking peace, tranquility and vitality in all aspects of their lives.

Tehran is a city with a distinct aroma, full of noise and countless colorful light bulbs and flags in all colors! When I first saw a row of yellow flags, immediately I asked my brother: "What country's flag could that be? That bright yellow! "

He pointed to the other flags, all in bright colors; red, blue, green, orange and purple, explaining to me that the flags were raised by the *shahrdari*, or municipal administration. "The *shahrdari* likes to decorate the whole town with flags and colorful light bulbs," he said. I noticed the brightly colored lights everywhere, even in the places where they didn't belong or were displayed in ill-matched combinations.

Each of the city's districts houses several mosques, many of which exhibit very beautiful architecture including golden, emerald or azure cupolas and minarets. I enjoy hearing the *azan* (the call to pray) at noon and at sunset, and the calls for donations. People are always welcome at the mosques, day and night and congregate there often. Sometimes the visitors will receive a cup of tea or a snack at during their stay at the mosques. For some women, the mosques can serve as a hangout spot, or refuge.

Men and women use the separate sections within the mosque. Sometimes they spend the whole day at the mosque praying, crying, and discussing different issues, reading *Quran*, exchanging info and finding friends, or even purchasing subsidized commodities.

Iranians are friendly, extroverted, sociable, and communicative, but very sensitive. Their emotion unfortunately can easily switch from love to hostility. They are often megalomaniacal. They like to play boss and lionize themselves. A doorman thinks he's the director, a nurse thinks she's the head physician and demands corresponding respect.

Women like conversations. They distinctly prefer a nice dialogue or window-shopping at a mall to sport. They love fashion. Some are fashion-obsessed and follow the latest trends as much as they can, even if fashionable clothes do not suit them at all. It makes them feel that they belong to the modern world.

Iranians aren't Arabs. We are Persians, but are surrounded by a handful of Arabian countries. This distinction is important to Iranians, and as such, they don't like to hear someone attribute them as Arabs.

Persia or Iran?

Today's state of Iran was called „Persia"until December 27th, 1934. On this day, then-ruling Shah Reza Pahlavi decreed the renaming. „Iran" means „land of the Aryans", with the Aryans being a native people that lived in the Persian-Indian region thousands of years ago – contrary to the false use of the term by the Nazis.

Persia? Iran? What is the correct term to use? What is the most common? If you ask a Persian what country he is coming from, the immediate answer usually is from Persia. The term Persia is reminiscent of the period of the glorious Persian Empire, but "Iran" is usually associated with the unpleasant recent political upheaval and the hostility with the West. Iran is also often confused with Iraq and associated with bloody conflict. I am confident that most Iranians would vote for Persia as their country's name.

Tehran is a multifaceted city, crazy and loud. The streets are packed with millions of vehicles and the never-ending streams of people. You can see even traffic jams at night. The city is unusually colorful. There is quite a lot of out-of-place and anachronistic architectural building styles next to one another along with the broad boulevards and romantic alleys. In the North, one sees the most beautiful and state-of-the-art buildings, restaurants and cafés, ultramodern shopping centers, parks and gardens, magnificent museums and palaces. In the South, there are impressive old buildings with handmade colorful mosaics and splendid architecture, bazars, museums, and old cafés. Every Friday a flea market called (*jomehbazar*) attracts hundreds of the tourists and the native. There are a lot of stores where you can buy the fresh nuts and the colorful spices for cheaper prices compare to the Northern part of the town.

In the south of Tehran, there is a center for everything: glasses, spices, mobile phones, furniture, and TV sets. The taxi drivers know this place well, but you can't be stingy with them. If you give the driver a generous tip right from the start, they will advise you correctly and in the end you'll have saved a lot of time and money. Taxi drivers are either married with a lot of children or they are students trying to pay tuition, so tips are important. On the other hand, the taxi fees are a real bargain compared to the West.

Over the years, the city has undergone groundbreaking changes with the new highways and subways system. That is a true metamorphosis. The city becomes grander, more beautiful and modern year after year. In Tehran people say "Iran is the capital of Tehran. "

Azadi Monument in Teheran

Great Bazar of the Zaid Mosque, in Teheran

Travelling in Iran

In Europe, when it is cloudy or gloomy, or when the hazy shade of winter lingers for a long time, people travel far to see the sunshine, even to another continent. In Iran, it takes only 40 minutes to fly, or eight hours by train, to the sunny Persian Gulf. If you yearn for snow and skiing, you need to drive only for 30 minutes out of the city toward the mountains to enjoy a completely different climate. Persia warmly and affectionately welcomes you.

Persia is always worth visiting, no matter what season. Iran is eight times bigger than Germany. One can enjoy winter at the Caspian Sea in the north, its sublime, exalted and breathtaking sceneries and summer at the Persian Gulf in the south just one hour flight away. In between, there are plenty of small and big cities with their own cultural and historical backgrounds. There is also a vast stretch of mysterious and exotic desert to explore.

Isfahan is half of the world. What does this mean? Where is it located? Majestic Isfahan; the previous capital city of Safavid dynasty established by Shah Abas the first (1501-1736) who left an astonishing cultural legacy, is a wonderful city with magnificent architecture. The vast "Imam Square" complex, the second largest square in the world, attracts a large number of people who come to see the magnificent palace of the kings, the majestic grand mosque and the intriguing long Bazar. It is especially busy on Fridays.

It is said that the people of Isfahan are particularly thrifty and business-minded. I always enjoy hearing Isfahanian accent. It's a pity that foreigners can't recognize this sweet, tuneful, and likable accent. Whenever I visit Isfahan, I make any excuse to talk to people to entertain myself. I ask for an address when I don't need it, I ask for change money or I go shopping, just to talk to them. Their accent is amusing and unique.

Isfahan is well known for its exceptional bridges

Qeshm Island	The island of Qeshm (that means „long island") is located in the Strait of Hormus in the Persian Gulf. There are many fishing villages here, historic buildings and the Hara mangrove forests, home to a lot of animal species, particularly birds.
Dasht-e Kavir	Iran has several desert areas. Particularly notable is Dasht-e Kavir, the Great Salt Desert on the Iranian plateau. There are tourist programs to explore Kavir desert, but given the extreme temperatures, travelers should abstain from visiting the desert during the summer months.
Yazd	One of the oldest and most beautiful cities in Iran. It is famous for its wind catchers that serve to provide the town's houses with cool air. It is also well known for being a place where fine silk and beautiful carpets come from. The running water in the buildings comes from the mountains and is being transported to the city via an antique canal system. Yazd is completely built from adobe and thus features a unique color. One can walk for hours in the many narrow alleys of the Old Town.
Qazvin	Qazvin is located in a distance of some 180 kilometers from Tehran. The city's history goes back several thousand years and there are a lot of historic buildings here, for example the magnificent Jameh Mosque, which for the most part dates back to the 12th century, other parts are even older.
Hamadan	A metropolis in western Iran, where the tomb of the great scholar Ibn Sina (Avicenna) is located. The tomb of biblical Esther is also here and many Jews went on a pilgrimage to see it. In Hamadan province, a short way out of town, there is the Ali Sadr cave. This is a cave system that's millions of years old and it's filled with water so there are boating tours available to explore the caves.
Susa	Located in the South, near the Persian Gulf, the town of Susa is not only Iran's oldest city but also one of the oldest continuously inhabited cities in the world, it was first mentioned in the Bible. Because of the summer heat, Susa should best be visited in the winter time. The town is really fascinating: if you descend one of the many stairs, you will literally find yourself in the past and you can visit the subterranean graves.

City of Yazd

Amir Chakhmaq Complex in Yazd

Lifestyle

Persians admire good looking, classy, dapper and stylish people. If you're going to a job interview, it is very important how you dress, what brand of watch you wear and what model of mobile phone you carry. Women make sure to wear an elegant coat and a unique headscarf from well-known brands such as Hermès or Versace.

Iranians usually look good and sometimes I think if there was not so much bias or bigotry against Iranians, the most beautiful actors and actresses, models, show hosts and many other stars could be from there. We have many George Clooneys and a lot of Angelina Jolies.

Persia is the land of poetry. Although Iranians are creative and talented in many fields, when it comes to poetry, it truly flows in the veins of these people. Poetry runs in my family: my mom, my aunt, my sisters and my friends, all have this flair. My father deeply loved rhyming. Even in stores you can often hear Persians spice their conversations with poems.

The most valuable thing about Persia is not the oil and the gas resources nor the other natural mines and cultural sites. No, it's the people who are the true treasure of the country.

The Persian people are ambitious, diligent, flexible and resilient. How often have other countries attempted to bring them to their knees; Greeks, Romans, Arabs, Turks, Mongols, later Russians, British, French and Americans? Persians have always got back on their feet.

When I am invited somewhere and the hosts learn that I live abroad, they would happily offer me their self-crafted beer and wine out of politeness. Production, consumption or sale of any alcoholic beverage is strictly prohibited in Iran. That's why many people make their own beer and wine at home. The non-Iranian-hosts see us as the inveterate drinkers, a presumption that stems from the freedom to purchase and consume alcohol abroad. The beer Persians produce at home may smell and look like beer, but it tastes more like a juice with lots of sugar.

Homemade wine looks like wine too, but it smells more like vinegar and it tastes as horrible as the beer. It's always amusing when the hosts make me taste the fermented juice as they excitedly and impatiently awaiting my verdict. They expect of course compliments and praise. What am I supposed to tell them? Would I risk my health by drinking these beverages?

I remember calling a friend once. A man answered the phone then I asked him to put my girlfriend on. He said laughingly: "Please talk to me as if I was your friend, I would listen and give you advice, just as your girlfriend would do. " It was when I recognized that I'd dialed the wrong number. He had taken the time to crack a joke, and tremendously amuse himself on it.

My sister-in-law likes my voice, and one day, when I began singing for her, she opened all windows to let the neighbors hear my voice and enjoy it too. A few minutes later, her neighbor came over with a plate full of pastries which made me really happy. In Germany, I don't really dare to practice because I am afraid that the neighbors might visit me with a police officer rather than with pastries.

In general, nowadays Iranians are becoming more materialistic and business-minded. They could probably sell a refridgerator to an Eskimo. The response of the Iranians to the rhetorical question, whether knowledge is more important or wealth, would be likely wealth.

Everywhere in the world, there are two decisive and clear_answers of *"yes"* or *"no"*, but in Iran there is a third additional option too: "Please stop by, we'll find a way. " And they indeed do find a way even if it looks futile or impossible at first. There's no absolute*"no"* specifically when it comes to business. There is always a solution, a remedy, a way.

Once when I expressed my misgivings and concern to an Iranian about new sanctions against Iran on the import of technology, food, drugs and medicine, he said in a calm and relaxed tone: "Don't be sad, Persians will always find a way. They just need a little time." For this endurance, I have deep respect for them.

Persians like shopping, they barely save. They like to show off what they have with pride. They always want to have the best and the newest brand of the items. This makes the country an ideal place for trade, an optimal market for the import and export business. If you are invited somewhere in Tehran, you will often hear "The cake is from the best pastry shop in Tehran. The tea is of the highest quality. The meat is from the most trustworthy butcher and the fruit are from the best garden in Tehran." Only the best matters. This is also why German products are very popular.

Persians talk a lot, gossip a lot, and are nosey. They have a keen fondness and interest in meddling in things they have no business in. They tell lies every once in a while and then try hard to convince you that they were nothing but truth by swearing tirelessly on it. They are stubborn and sensitive. They often rant and possess a large vocabulary of curse words fitting to each situation. They ask frequently personal questions which have nothing to do with them, such as; how old are you? Are you married? Where do you live? Do you have kids? They just want to poke their nose in every single detail of the other people's lives. Privacy has no meaning to them. Mostly, they don't have even a notion of it. They also don't like any negative prediction, for example, when it comes to a premonition of an earthquake in Tehran or the reports about an epidemic, they don't want to hear because they think they cannot change or influence it.

Iranians love music. Indeed, they are music-obsessed. Music can be heard everywhere: in taxi, in stores and in restaurants. Even you see babies moving back and forth in rhythm with music, beaming and smiling without teeth. The construction workers bring their tape recorders in the morning to make their hard jobs enjoyable and sometimes they sing along loudly. It sounds nice when passing by, especially when a good voice permeates the air, and the neighbors will reward them for it with a warm meal.

A gathering usually comes to an end with music. After dinner people sit together and enjoy music while trying to make sure everyone feels well. Even in a remembrance of a beloved person, the relatives and friends after the ritual will sing music or poems chorally in a calm and serene atmosphere. The magnificent lyrics of prominent and world famous Persian poets will be recited, for example those poems and verses of Hafez, Omar Khayyam, Saadi, Firdausi and other famous names. Naturally, the kids are always around making their own poetry, learning and expressing Persian arts and culture from their earliest days.

Persians love the bibliomancy. Many of them start their days with a poem of omnibus of Hafez. They close their eyes, pray for blessing of his soul and open his volume of poems with the eyes still closed. The poem chosen this way is read aloud. They believe that the poet's soul has the ability to foretell all events of the upcoming days through his poems. Persians believe deeply in the mystery behind read poems becoming reality.

Poems by Hafez are dynamic and optimistic; they give the reader hope and positive energy. In almost every single household there is a Hafez poetry volume. After calling upon him loudly Persians say *"rohat shad"* means "May your soul rest in peace" or "May your soul be in joy and happiness".

I am amused tremendously when the Persians dance the Tango. They have improvised this dance by reducing it to moving back and forth with very slow steps, all without the correct hand, arm, shoulder and head postures. On top of that, they step on each other's feet all the time. I believe that Iran is the only country where you can dance Tango without taking any dancing lessons. The way they dance Tango could be any type of dancing except Tango, but they are very content and satisfied with their dancing skill. They calling it"Tango Iranian Style".

Persians are proud of their glorious, ancient medicine. The first doctor and surgeon, Ibn Sina, hailed from Persia, and was known in Europe by the Latinized name "Avicenna". He became well known to a broader public through the Noah Gordon novel "The Physician". He lived from 980 to 1037 and not only did he make a name for himself as the father of Persian medicine and surgery, but he was a universally educated scholar who also published philosophical writing. Furthermore, he authored the "Book of Healing" which is not only about medicine, but also about psychology, astronomy and other sciences.

Most Iranian parents wish for their children to become doctors. There are many other famous scientists from Persia, but no other profession has a reputation nearly as good as the doctor's.

Doctor al-Razi was born near Tehran in 865. He discovered alcohol, the base for all alcoholic beverages. Razi passed away impoverished. Alcohol is now, of course, a source of great income for many, even as an important raw material to manufacture the various fragrances so desired by women.

Omar Khayam was the inventor of one of the most precise calendar to the current day, it's called *"Jalali Calendar"*. Undoubtedly, for the Germans who are well-known for the characteristic of punctuality, this achievement should have been a significant and impressive invention.

Persians are looking with great pride at their history, arts and culture. Known in Western literature as Cyrous, the ancient Emperor Kouroush established the first declaration of human rights in 538 B.C. He ruled over the Great Empire of Persia, and now many Persian families name their sons after him out of gratitude and respect.

One of my brothers has the same name "Kourosh". He works as a Nephrologist in Berlin and his knowledge of Persian culture and history is deep. He is well aware of the responsibility that his name's heritage carries and tries to act accordingly.

He told me about a conversation with a patient who had been admitted to the hospital in very critical condition. The patient anxiously had asked him about his country of origin. "I am Persian" my brother calmly said. Passionately the patient had taken his hands "Doctor, I am glad, I'm in safe hands with you."

In Iran, parents always choose meaningful names for their children, favoring classic names over modern ones. They believe strongly that names play a big role in the success and luck in their children's lives. Someone called "Kourosh" will have completely different character and attitude from someone who is called Gholam; an Arabian name stands for "slave" or "servant" in religious term.

Anecdotally, I see this in comparing the names and the life paths of people whom I knew. I had once a friend whose first name was Dana which means "savvy" and she was the best in her class in school. Another one was called Diana that was the goddess of hunting, and she indeed became a hunter. The other funny example is my mother's dermatologist who is called Poosti, which means "relating to skin" in Persian.

There are many more examples and a lot of other pretty first names. Darius was a Persian king in the fifth century B.C., Jasmin is the flower and the symbol of love, Shirin means "sweet, beautiful, pleasant one" and Anush or Anushka means "immortal, eternal". My first name is actually Susan Dokht and that's an ancient monarchal name, so a channel to my princess title. I think I am the only European princess with Persian background.

In my opinion, it falls upon parents to give their children meaningful names, the names that would have a positive impact on the children's way of lives or imply something about the family's' heritage.

Persians love warm and cozy rooms. When I came to Germany, I experienced the cold to my bone like never before. Everywhere was chilling cold for me. Whenever the rooms were finally warm enough to my horror, some German rushed in, opened the doors and windows again saying: *"Wir brauchen frische Luft."* "We need fresh air." To my view, that was anything but warm and cozy!

Now the story's turned. In the course of life, I've become used to German habits. I am as a person who has grown up in Germany appreciating the value of the fresh air, and now whenever I come back to Tehran the first thing I would do is to open the doors and windows saying: *"We need fresh air."* Unfortunately, often that's not possible, so to avoid arguments, I prefer just to step outside, despite the air pollution in Tehran. Indeed, the air in Tehran is rather devoid of oxygen, and there is little fresh air.

When I traveled to Cyprus with my children a few years ago, I saw people swimming in the sea, although it was early May. I went to the tour guide to ask whether the water was warm enough to get in with my children. She responded by asking what country we were from. Before I got a chance to answer, she said, "Oh, Germany. You can go swimming. For everyone else, the water is too cold. The people you see in the sea are all from Germany." Seemingly it was clear to her that we were from Germany.

My siblings

I have four brothers. All of them are medical Doctor Specialists. They live scattered in Tehran, Berlin, Bern and Los Angeles. They pursue their profession with a lot of dedication and continue their education even now. They are always well-informed about everything. I like calling them "living Encyclopedias". If I have a question about politics, economy or history, I will call them, particularly my brother who lives in Switzerland, because he is easier to reach and explains everything to me with simple words and joy. He is sometimes even quicker than Google.

He has always a great sense of humor. Once he told me an anecdote:

During his night shift at the hospital where he worked as an eye surgeon, a patient came in at midnight. My brother had expected that night to be quiet but this patient came in with a needle in his eye. My brother took care of him and with a smile "Body, this late at night people are either in bed or in a concert, in a movie theater or spending some cozy time with their friends. Please tell me, for Christ's sake, how a needle got into your eye?" he asked him. The patient begged my brother not to make him laugh, because then it would hurt even more.

Another brother is an anesthetist in Los Angeles. One night, he got home late and extremely tired. He was sitting next to his girlfriend who had spent all day at home, and she asked him to tell her something funny to make her laugh. Badgered by the persistent pleases of his girlfriend, my brother said placidly, in his pleasant voice, "Make you laugh? Honey, still you do not know what I do? I am an anesthetist. I put people to sleep for a living."

My sister had once enrolled in a women's swimming competition and I accompanied her. We were brimming over with excitement and were wondering how well she would do.

My mom waited anxiously for us at home. We took her high expectations with us. She always wanted to see us as successful and as winners, nothing less. She told us stories about success all the time when we were young, and still does, although we all aren't young anymore. Like many Iranians, she adheres to the proverb is "Learn from the cradle to the grave. It's never too late to learn something."

Having arrived at the stadium, we learned only four candidates including my sister took part at the competition. It was still in doubt whether with that low number of participants the competition would be held at all. After long discussions back and forth, the competition was given a green light to go ahead. My sister was very anxious because of my mom high expectations. She was determined to win. She jumped too quickly though, and unfortunately ended up being disqualified.

When we got home, she was completely quiet. I didn't dare to say anything. Nobody knew but me that there had been only four participants in the competition including my sister. No sooner had we stepped into the home than mom with a big question mark on her face began to interrogate us. Suddenly, my sister found her voice again and with utter self-confidence loudly said: "Mom, mom, I won third runner up! I stood fourth."

My mom nodded, looked down at the ground "Well...Okay, fourth isn't that bad, at least you didn't fail the competition." she said. I smiled stealthily. (My sister is now a top-notch Engineer.) Maybe my mom would know the truth after reading this book.

A few years ago, when I visited my sister Katayoun in America, I was watching her walking to her car early in the morning to go at work. Her little son Ario was looking at his mother through the window; suddenly he opened the window and started to cry.

My mom took him in her arms, "Dear Ario, your mom must go to work to be able to take care of you, to buy you nice toys and to take you to Disneyland one of these days. She needs to earn money for all that and that's why she has to go to work."

"Go! Go mom! Go faster please! "Ario yelled out through the window.

Believe me, all Iranians have good sense of humor and my family is no exception. Usually from the first moment I board the plane, I am being amused until I am back in Germany.

I have no clue how Persians have so much energy, humor and zest for life, in spite of facing so many problems in all aspects of life.

Chewing gum as currency

Time and time again, I get amused when Persian shopkeepers give me chewing gum, matches or chocolate instead of the change due at a supermarket checkout, as if these small items would belong to the national currency. At any pharmacy, you'll sometimes get Band-Aids as change or cough drops even if you're not coughing. Everyone knows the prices for chocolate and chewing gum and accepts this method. Not only have I never seen anyone complaining about it, but to the contrary, they seem content and even convinced that it would help cut down the time waiting in queue. Most of people have a basket full of such small "change currency" items instead in our kitchens.

I see in this customary practice an intelligent improvisation; a way to make daily life and business less complicated. There is patience here. I can well imagine what a riot would break out in Germany if someone tried to apply this approach at the check out register: "What's that? I didn't buy this! What am I supposed to do with chewing gum? Where's my change? "

The movies

Going to Movie Theater in Tehran can be a story in itself.

Many Persian movies are not only aestheitically beautiful but also layered and nuanced with sophistication in order to meet strict censorship laws. They might be seen from a European perspective as slow-paced and monotonous; they seemingly continue to go on forever without major events. Nothing happens for minutes at a time, the cameras move very slowly and you need patience to watch a film to the end. If you pay attention to the hidden messages behind the story, however, it is often bold, exciting and thought provoking.

Recently someone recommended a Persian movie to me. I found it and was so excited to watch it. I switched off my phone and began to watch enthusiastically but I could only stand a few minutes of it and turned it off. It was too sad, boring and uneventful. Only a few scenes had music, and the rest of the movie passed in absolute silence. A few weeks later, I ran into the person who had recommended the movie to

Persian Films

Persian movies have frequently received outstanding reviews at international film festivals in the recent past. Iranian filmmakers such as Jafar Panahi, Majid Majidi, Asghar Farhadi or Abbas Kiarostami are often praised for the artful standards of their works and receive awards.

me. When we we talked about it, I found out that I'd completely misunderstood the movie and missed out the hidden point of it.

Persian movies often deal with social issues; they give viewers tips and advice and share the mundane intimacies of life experiences. Sexual or erotic scenes, even hugs, are forbidden, so all the emotions and sentiments must be conveyed to the viewers by the innocent words or the facial expressions.

Nevertheless, the movie theaters are very popular and are well attended. When I was sitting in a movie theater in Tehran for the first time in many years, I wondered why the interior lights wouldn't go out the way that I knew from Germany. Leaving the light on is a disturbance after all, because it doesn't let you see the movie screen well. But no, in Tehran the lights are intentially left on. There are even small lamps at the front and rear ends of each row of seats to prevent lovers from getting too close to each other, holding hands or even cuddling. I found it strange.

Necessity is the mother of invention

One day, when I wanted to buy some nuts in Tehran my brother told me, "Before buying give the vendor a good tip, otherwise you'll get old or even moldy nuts."

I followed his advice and to my wonder, the vendor didn't take the old nuts from the display, but he fetched the fresh ones all the way from the basement.

I don't blame the vendors for doing that. They use any opportunity to increase the small incomes that feed their families. The ailing economy has made them both vulnerable and inventive, so they create their own ways to survive. The same things can be observed at markets of all kinds of fresh food such as fruit, vegetables, meat or fish.

Arguing

Unfortunately, I admit the fact that in Iran conversations often turn into arguing and furious discussion. Beware if that happens, it will be hard to dissuade either party involved in the argument from his/her belief or perspective. It is likely they will end up hurling a barrage of curses to each other before they leave. The best way to keep away from such arguments is not to insist on your opinion. It is better just to smile and hold back your thoughts to yourself. Try listen and to steer the conversation to another topic!

Moreover, you shouldn't take everything literally.

Once I got almost slapped on the face by a relative with an ill mood when I repeatedly questioned him, "Are you serious? Do you really mean that? Really! " He answered angrily, "Of course I'm serious. First of all, I am a man! Secondly, have I ever said something that was not true? Am I a liar?"

In Iran, men might get offended or feel insulted when they are being questioned repeatedly by women. They think they have an automatic right just because they are men.

Persians are also peevish and touchy, which can often push them to abandon logic.

Gosh! It is really not easy to live in two worlds with different cultures and mentalities. When I came to Germany, my spouse constantly urged me to make eye contact with the other in a conversation. He emphasized that eye contact could help me better connect with others. On the contrary, in Iran it is polite for a woman to avoid looking into the eyes of an unfamiliar man that she is having a conversation with. It might even sometimes be considered quite rude or be taken in a wrong way by the man.

Even as I become more accustomed to the customs in Germany, I still feel German when I am in Iran and like a Persian when I am in Germany.

Words and poems

My siblings and I were often picked up from school by my father. Sometimes he took us to a movie theater, museum or bookstore.

My father would pick some books and before drowning in those books for minutes and forgetting everything around him, he gave us some books to thumb through too.

His library at home was almost filled to capacity with books by Persian personalities, such as Firdausi, Saadi, Hafis, Khayam, Molana, Ganjawi, and Shamse Tabrizi and so on.

Saadi

Saadi, born around 1210, is considered to be the father of poems. At the entrance of the United Nations building, these lines written by him can be read:

The sons of Adam are limbs of each other,
having been created of one essence.
When the calamity of time affects one limb,
the other limbs cannot remain at rest.
If you have no sympathy for the troubles of others,
you are unworthy to be called by the name of a human.

As children, we got to know writers, poets and their works one by one as our father introduced them to us. Our father's adoration of the books made us so much more curious to learn what was in them. His favorite poet was Saadi. I hold the memory of those short trips with my father dearly, and still find inspiration in them.

Johann Wolfgang von Goethe

Excerpts from „West-Eastern Divan", inspired by Hafez:

God's very own the Orient!
God's very own the Occident!
The North land and the Southern land
Rest in the quiet of His hand.

****

Whence Hafiz, as I dare suppose
A place beside thee I have won
For when men's thoughts together run
Between the men a likeness grows.

****

O Hafiz, from thy songs I learn
The way that poets should be praised
Behold! To thee I make return
And nobly let the thanks be raised!

****

Ah! Let the whole world slide and sink,
Hafiz, with thee alone the strife
Of song I seek. Twin brothers we
Our pain, our pleasure common be!
Like thee to love, like thee to drink,
Shall be my pride, shall be my life.

Persia, land of poets and storytellers

Hafez: Hafez was born in Shiraz, a large town in southern Iran in 1315. Hafez was an inspiration for the famous German poet Johann Wolfgang von Goethe. *Divan*, Hafez' work best known outside of Iran, served as orientation point for Goethe for his poems in the „West-eastern divan" collection. The German town of Weimar has a monument of two chairs facing one another. The chairs stand as symbols for Goethe's encounter with the works of Hafez, whom he once referred to as his „twin brother in mind". The monument had been dedicated by former Iranian president Khatami when he visited Germany.

Ferdowsi: Ferdowsi is considered to be the savior of the Persian language Farsi and he is a national hero for Iranians. He was born in 940 and lived in a time in which the religious rulers attempted to suppress the cultural identity of the Persians and instead wanted to enforce Arabian. Ferdowsi wrote countless poems by which he managed to preserve Persian history, language and culture and to relay it to the next generations. His masterpiece is called „Schahnameh", this book can be found in every Persian household.

Rumi: Rumi enjoys so much popularity and fame that many countries claim he originally derives from there, including Turkey, Tajikistan and Afghanistan. But he is Persian; all of his poems are in the Persian language. After the Arabs had attacked Iran he fled the country and moved to Konya, Turkey. There, he created his works and he has also been buried there. Rumi's tomb in Konya is a mecca for the poet's fans.

Rumi: „The Reed Flute's song"

Hearken to the reed-flute, how it complains, lamenting its banishment from its home:

Ever since they tore me from my osier bed, my plaintive notes have moved men and women to tears.

I burst my breast, striving to give vent to sighs, And to express the pangs of my yearnings for my home.

He who abides far away from his home is ever longing for the day he shall return.

My wailing is heard in every throng in concert with them that rejoice and them that weep.

Each interprets my notes in harmony with his own feelings, but not one fathoms the secrets of my heart.

My secrets are not alien from my plaintive notes, yet they are not manifest to the sensual eye and ear.

Body is not veiled from soul, neither soul from body, yet no man hath ever seen a soul.

This plaint of the flute is fire, not mere air. Let him who lacks this fire be accounted dead!

'Tis the fire of love that inspires the flute, 'Tis the ferment of love that possesses the wine.

The flute is the confidant of all unhappy lovers; Yea, its strains lay bare my inmost secrets..

Who hath seen a poison and an antidote like the flute? Who hath seen a sympathetic consoler like the flute?

The flute tells the tale of love's bloodstained path; it recounts the story of Majnun's love toils.

None is privy to these feelings save one distracted, as ear inclines to the whispers of the tongue.

Through grief my days are as labor and sorrow, my days move on, hand in hand with anguish.

Yet, though my days vanish thus, 'tis no matter, do thou abide, O Incomparable Pure One!

But all who are not fishes are soon tired of water; and they who lack daily bread find the day very long

So the " Raw " comprehend not the state of the "Ripe;" therefore it behooves me to shorten my discourse.

Arise, O son! Burst thy bonds and be free! How long wilt thou be captive to silver and gold?

Though thou pour the ocean into thy pitcher, it can hold no more than one day's store.

The pitcher of the desire of the covetous never fills, the oyster-shell fills not with pearls till it is content.

Only he whose garment is rent by the violence of love is wholly pure from covetousness and sin.

Hail to thee, then, O love, sweet madness! Thou who healest all our infirmities!

Who are the physician of our pride and self-conceit! Who art our Plato and our Galen!

Love exalts our earthly bodies to heaven, and makes the very hills to dance with joy!

O lover, 'twas love that gave life to Mount Sinai, when it quaked, and Moses fell down in a swoon.

Did my Beloved only touch me with his lips, I too, like the flute, would burst out in melody.

But he, who is parted from them that speak his tongue, though he possesses a hundred voices, is perforce dumb.

When the rose has faded and the garden is withered, the song of the nightingale is no longer to be heard.

The Beloved is all in all, the lover only veils Him; the Beloved is all that lives, the lover a dead thing.

When the lover feels no longer Love's quickening, he becomes like a bird who has lost its wings. Alas!

How can I retain my senses about me, when the Beloved shows not the light of His countenance?

Love desires that this secret should be revealed, for if a mirror reflects not, of what use is it?

Knowest thou why thy mirror reflects not? Because the rust has not been scoured from its face.

O friends, ye have now heard this tale, which sets forth the very essence of my case.

Taxi, Taxi

There are many stories to tell about taxis and taxi drivers in Tehran. There are two kinds of taxis: The private taxis and the group taxis, both of which have different rates of services.

Once I flew to Tehran after a long time and there was nobody available to pick me up at the airport, so I had to take a taxi. Even from far away, I could see a lot of men standing in a group at the taxi stand, drinking tea, smoking, making jokes and waiting for passengers. They didn't let a minute pass by without telling each other hilarious jokes, talking about anecdotes or sharing experiences. I think they try to forget about the exhausting work conditions, the traffic jams and the stinky and stuffy air. They often aren't even covered by any kind of health insurance.

It is no wonder that you can find some good psychologists among them, as they possess a great deal of knowledge pertaining to human nature. They quickly become aware if a passenger is living in Iran or overseas. If they recognize you as a tourist, they will instantly prearrange a week's schedule of activities and places that you should experience if you're in town. They aren't stingy, and they don't withhold their information. They will tell you what is really going on in society, where to go, what to see, and where to eat the best and most authentic foods. They hand out these pieces of advices without asking the passenger if they want to hear it at all. They just start talking.

To the best of their ability, all questions and special requests will be answered, including "Where can I buy the best caviar or saffron? Which merchant offers the most beautiful rugs for a reasonable price?" No problem. Nobody can answer these questions better than Tehran's taxi drivers.

It is incredibly difficult and sometimes rather dangerous to drive on your own through Tehran's streets. The taxi drivers often call themselves "Schumacher of Germany," but you cannot praise them too much, otherwise they will start driving backwards on the freeway. I experienced that once. Believe it or not, I don't have the guts to drive in Tehran for even five minutes. In general, traffic in Iran is perilous. There are probably traffic rules and regulations, but they are treated at best as recommendations rather than obligations. If you choose to drive in Tehran, keep your eyes open and don't panic. There can be six cars side by side on a four-lane road in Tehran. Be prepared for incessant honking, even when it is absolutely unnecessary. You can see cars breaking down all the time, as there are many old and unreliable vehicles on the roads.

Generally speaking, smaller car accidents are resoloved among the drivers; sometimes with money, sometimes with the exchange of a few profanities. Some older drivers, like my father want to avoid trouble and just say, "Drive on!" It's better than waiting for the police to get through the traffic jams to get to you.

Once when I was sitting in a taxi, I noticed a large hole on the taxi's floor. I was so worried that my shoes or purse would fall into it. Being scared, I informed the driver who answered me with a simple smile, "repairing that hole costs me too much money. You will find a small rug next to you; you can cover the hole with it."

Taxi drivers usually like listening to music while on the job, sometimes even singing along to it. However, they rarely ask the passengers whether or not they want to listen to the music. That can be quite annoying and disturbing, especially when you're tired or the driver has a horrible singing voice.

The drivers can recognize you as a tourist by the way you slam the door. Why? Because natives know that the doors are very light and flimsy, so they close them with care. That's entirely different in Germany, where a taxi is usually a Mercedes or another big car with heavy doors. A taxi driver once told me, "If you bang the doors this way two more times, then all the doors will fall off!" You have to shut the doors softly, because the cars are often really old and dilapidated.

Cab drivers provide all kinds of services: they go shopping, change currencies, or even if a passenger has forgotten something somewhere, they will drive to that destination; ask, search, and investigate until they have found the lost item. If necessary, they even wait for the passenger until he or she returns. If an order is urgent, they will order a motorcyclist who is faster.

I have depended on taxi drivers in Tehran many times, and am grateful for the help they have provided. I remember once in a big mall I wanted to buy a purse, but I didn't have enough money on me, so I sent the taxi to my mom and waited with my new purse for the taxi driver to return. He came back with quite a bit of money. Then, he waited for his scanty taxi fee. I had trusted him even though I didn't know anything about him. Not his name, the company he worked for, or any other information. He just came back with the money. They are so honest and trustworthy. They believe that honesty and hard work will put religiously blessed food on the table for their families. You often find the most beautiful proverbs on their car windows about life, love, and faith in God. Sometimes, you'll see a taxi driver's entire family album inside his cab on the doors. I gain a lot of pleasure from reading these epigrams and looking at their pictures.

It is said that taxi drivers usually act completely uninhibited and unrestrained when there is a passenger on board, acting as if they were alone in the car. They will talk on the phone loudly, talk about their private lives, and they won't care much about whether or not the passenger might be disturbed by it. I think that it's dangerous to talk on the cell phone while driving in that heavy and chaotic traffic.

What I find very interesting and humorous is the money bills seen on the compartments, dashboards, panels, basically everywhere inside the taxis. In order to finish their transactions as quickly as possible, the taxi drivers sort their bills by value and place them at hand to make them easier to access: the large ones above the rearview mirror or behind the sunscreen, and the smaller ones you will find in the cigarette lighter or in the compartments of the car.

Tehran is an incredibly crowded and sprawling city, an unusual, unique and incomparable metropolis. It is often not easy to find an address. Although the taxi drivers do not use GPS devices, they will find every address and destination themselves. They safely transport their passengers everywhere and help them out in any way that they can. I have a lot of respect for them.

Buses

Buses in Iran meet the most current international standards and are rarely older than ten years. They are all equipped with air conditioners. In the city buses, men and women travel separately. In fact, seats are divided into two sections, with the gentlemen siting in the front rows and the ladies in the back. In the middle of the bus a metal bar divides the area for men and women. Women and men board through separate entrances and exits. Young single men and women like to stand and ogle each other in the middle of the bus.

Specifically, in the mornings, the front areas of the buses are often empty because many of the men are already at work. The rear section however is often bursting at the seams. So, many women have to stand if they don't quickly find a seat, sometimes with small children in their arms or many shopping bags in their hands. By now, some women, mostly older ones, have had the audacity to break the rules by crossing underneath the bar and taking a seat in the section reserved for men, and the bus drivers never complain about that.

Once, when I was sitting in the first row of a bus, in the women's section of course, a woman with two large bags got in the bus. She put one of her bags on my lap and said,

"Please hold my bag for a few minutes." Then, she proceeded to open the other bag and presented her goods for sale. She was selling underwear.

She pulled one piece after another from her bag, presenting bras, panties, thongs and stockings in all sizes and colors. The women cautiously looked at the underwear that they were being offered, but they hardly dared to ask any questions pertaining to the quality of the goods, or to touch the items to feel the fabric. Maybe they were embarrassed. The saleswoman was yelling and announcing her spectacular prices for the bras.

How can you try on a bra on a bus? How could a woman be able to decide whether something fits her or not in front of all those people? Some women donated money to the vendor without buying anything because they wanted to support the young woman.

There are often cases where various items are being offered for purchase on the busses. Sometimes, small children will get on the bus and ask passengers to buy their products: paper towels, pillows, gloves, or anything else that they can carry in their small hands. However, they don't like answering passenger's questions, such as how old they are or why they are not at school.

In another situation, I was once sitting in the first row when a large box of cake was suddenly put into my lap by a woman who asked that I watch it carefully. Later, when the seat next to me became available, she took the seat, thanked me, and opened the box to offer me a piece of the cake. She insisted, "Please, take some! The cake is really tasty and fresh!"

When you enter a bus in Tehran, pause and consider whether you really want to sit in first row. As on an airplane in the exit row, you may be asked to assist other passengers. Surprisingly, not even once did I see someone complaining about it or being annoyed. People like to help. I'm truly amazed at their patience and kindness.

The tickets for a bus ride aren't necessarily purchased in advance as they are in Germany. You can pay for them in cash, and even after the ride. Because of this, someone is always standing in front of the door to collect the fare. Often, that person is not able to collect all the fares when a lot of passengers get off the bus at the same time. Sometimes no fare is taken from passengers who seem to not be able to afford it. In the instance where a co-driver does not have enough change on him or the whole process takes too long, a passenger might even offer to take care of the bus fare for a few people around him. In these situations, I see the genuine meaning of having empathy for others.

My dear compatriots: I love you. You have developed such a unique esprit de corps with your innovative mind, sympathy and humor. You have regulated everything in an unconventional, uncomplicated way among yourselves that makes it all easy. I feel pride in the blood that flows through my veins for being one of you.

Pedestrians

Tehran is a very crowded city and traffic is awful. Of course, there are pedestrian crosswalks in Tehran, but it doesn't automatically mean that the drivers will stop for pedestrians. Whoever is faster and braver has the right of way. It's like the old saying "the stronger will survive". If you have to cross the street, you should do it by any means, otherwise you will be standing on the other side forever and the cars will never stop for you. But keep in mind; you are at risk of getting severely injured or losing your life every time you cross the street. That's not a joke. My own uncles, both renowned international lawyers, were killed by hit and run drivers on two separate occasions as they were crossing the street. Was it just an accident? I will never know.

Apparently, whether or not the cars would stop for you or run you over depends on driver's mood or the appearance of the pedestrians. If you are not well dressed or look messy or untidy, good luck crossing the street in Tehran. One day, I was dressed up to go somewhere. When I was on my way at an intersection, a car stopped immediately in front of me and allowed me to cross the crossroad. Passing the intersection, I shouted out "thank you" to the young male driver for stopping and respecting my right as a pedestrian. "You're welcome... actually it depends on the pedestrian," he shouted back, to which I replied, "What?" He then replied, "There are Pedestrians, and there are pedestrians!" I was confused by his answer, but then I remembered that I had recently run into Mr. Tehrani, our old, overweight and kind of messy neighbor walking by with the help of a cane and a cast on his foot. When I asked him what had happened, he answered grumbling, "bi namusa (disrespectful assholes), I was run over by a car even though I was clearly walking in the pedestrian zone." He also added, "Sweetheart, in this city the streets are not safe as in Europe. Watch out carefully for the stupid cars, please!" It was at that moment when I figured out what the driver meant when he said, "It depends on the type of pedestrian…"

Intersection

One day, when I was carrying a number of bags, a policeman switched the traffic light to red the exact moment I arrived at an intersection. "Oh no, these bags are too heavy, I don't want to wait" I sighed. "No problem, I'll switch it back to green," he answered without a pause. Indeed, the light turned green at once and he even carried my shopping bags across the street.

Once, I was really looking forward to an appointment with a friend in Tehran. We had agreed to meet each other at a large intersection and wanted to go shopping and thereafter to go for a drink in a very small but super elegant café. We agreed on sharp 6 pm.

In Iran, women who are standing somewhere waiting alone are frowned upon, especially if that place is at an intersection. I was there in time and waited for a few minutes. As some drivers started honking and ogling at me and even some of them stopped shortly in front of me, I became nervous.

The situation was hardly bearable for me any longer. I walked up to the *Sarkarostowar* (traffic officer) and asked him if I could stand next to him in the middle of the intersection. I explained the officer my story. He nodded. A few minutes later he asked me if I had a mobile. "No, "I said. He said nothing.

When the traffic light turned green, he whistled and showed his stop sign to the first vehicle passing by. The driver pulled over at the shoulder of the street. Unlike in Germany, where you must remain sitting and wait in your car, he jumped out of the car like a flash.

"Sarkarostowar (that's what police officers are often called), what is my fault, did I drive too fast? Forgive me, I have an appointment, please let me drive on!" he said.

In Iran, smaller traffic offenses are often regulated with all kinds of tickets, and a lot of times it is sufficient to apologize and promise humbly that it won't happen again.

My dear *Sarkarostowar* asked him calmly if he had a mobile on him, and the stopped driver affirmed.

"Okay, good, please dial her friend's number" he prompted the driver and looked at me.

I gave her phone number to the stranger, and he then called her. He then asked about my friend's name in a serious manner, as if taking care of my problem had been the most normal thing in the world. Meanwhile, *Sarkarostowar* had completely forgotten his intersection. Chaos ensued behind him as he managed the driver helping me.

"Sepide, where are you? Miss Susan is waiting for you impatiently," the driver asked my friend.

Sepide answered that in ten minutes she would have been there. And since she didn't know who it was on the phone, she added that he was welcome to come along.

"No, thank you, I have my own plan, "the driver laughed. Then he asked me worriedly if there was anything else he could do for me. When I said no and expressed my gratitude, he said goodbye.

Finally, Sepide arrived, but unfortunately, she was driving in the opposite direction and U-turn was not allowed.

"Which direction do you have to go?" the policeman asked me.

"The opposite direction of the traffic stream and she must make a U-turn, but how and where? " I said.

Then he blew his whistle again, all motorists had to stop and allowed Sepide make her U-turn. Politely he opened the passenger door for me and wished us "God be with you. " There was no honking. Even I saw clearly the smile on some drivers' faces. My *Sarkarostowar* was manna from heaven to me.

When we passed the intersection, Sepide anxiously asked me about the guy on the phone. I took a deep breath and told her that I didn't know him at all.

This is how my compatriots are dealing with each other, despite of many problems. That's what I admire and love about them.

Tehran driver's license

To my best recollection, I passed the written test for my driver's license in Tehran successfully.

After a few hours of driving instructions and passing the written exam, I was permitted to take the city exam. Anxiously, I went to the Department of Motor Vehicles. I was determined to pass the city test on the first attempt. After a "Good morning" and handing over my documents, we got into the car and drove off.

There was a roundabout, actually a traffic circle, on the route, and I was supposed to enter it. The examiner wanted to see if I knew who had the right of way in a roundabout.

All of a sudden he yelled, "Do you see that large bill over there on the ground?" I nodded. He said excitedly that the color of the bill indicated that it was worth about 500 Euros!

"Okay. Drive faster," he said, "and do not pay attention this time to the right of way or the regulations! Stop next to the bill so that I can pick it up easily but inconspicuously! "

In that moment, all he was thinking about was that money left on the street and he had completely forgotten my driving test. That incident disturbed my focus on driving, and for a moment what I had learnt seemingly vanished from my mind. I was expected not to pay attention to the regulations and right of way. "Okay, I will do that. " I thought.

I drove over to the bill cautiously and prudently. Exactly the way he had asked me to do. I stopped next to the bill; he opened the door and picked it up gleefully. He let out a sigh of relief and put the money in his pocket.

"Of course you will get some of it too, "he said politely.

"Thank you, but it was you who spotted the bill and it was also your idea to go there in time to pick it up. That's why the money is yours. I don't want any share of it. "I answered promptly.

For a moment, he was silent. He probably was thinking "Thank God".

"Congratulations, you passed the test with honor. Where do you live? Can I give you a ride home? "He smiled at me cheerfully.

Now tell me, where else in the world can you pass a driving test "with honor"within just a few minutes on the first try and even be chauffeured home?

Taarof

In Iran, *"Taarof"* is a way of expressing the polite manners and etiquette that can be found everywhere, but I can't translate the word exactly. Unfortunately, it can sometimes lead to total confusion and entanglement that can rasp the nerves. There is no equivalent for this word in other languages, but to a certain degree the phrase "phoney complement" is close. I think an example can clarify this term much better.

Imagine you are in a store and you want to purchase something. If you ask for the price, you should not be surprised by this answer, "It costs nothing for you. You can take it and enjoy, later we talk about the price."

Or when you take a private taxi and at the destination you ask, "How much should I pay?" Then the taxi driver will answer, "For you, nothing."

But they don't mean it. In Iran, you cannot walk away without paying either. It is just considered the politeness and not talking about money right away. Certainly, for indigenous people it's pleasant to experience *"Taarof"*. Such words and behavior will warm the hearts, even though often it's not to be taken seriously.

Another example: A convivial host will certainly ask his guests if they like to get something to eat or drink, and the guests might initially answer, "No, thank you" although they are thirsty or maybe hungry. I think that could get on one's nerves, and often I don't know how to react.

A popular old story

Once, there was a wanderer.

He walked along a path one day and saw a snake that had been caught in a fire and it cried for help.

He took a stick and freed the snake from the flames.

The snake wound around his leg and said: „I will bite you. "

Upon that, the wanderer said: „The Good is followed by Good", but the snake said the opposite. They agreed to hike on together to ask a third about it.

They saw an old tree and told it about the incident and asked for its opinion. „Dear tree, what is the Good followed by? Good or bad? "

It said: „The Bad. People come to me, party and rest in my shade. When they leave me again, they leave their trash behind and their children snap off my branches and take them away. "

The wanderer and the snake walked on. They encountered a lake, told it about it all and asked for its opinion. It said: „The Good is followed by Bad. The humans are swimming in the lake, rest on my shores and when they leave me, they contaminate me and throw their trash into my water. "

The wanderer and the snake walked on and spotted a fox. They told it about the incident as well and asked for its verdict.

It said: „I cannot tell you like that, I have to experience the situation. "

So they lit a fire and threw the snake into it.

The wanderer again took his stick and tried to free the snake from the fire, but the fox averted the rescue and said to the wanderer: „You have seen how ungrateful it was to you. Let her die. "And it got scorched by the fire.

The wanderer hiked on and on his way encountered a hunter who was desperately looking for a prize. After the hunter had asked the wanderer whether he had seen a hare or a deer or some other game, the wanderer pointed to where he had come from and said: A few minutes ago I have seen a fox walk along this path."

Persian Cuisine

Many types of entertainment such as night clubs, discos, shows, foreign movies and other options are forbidden, so Persians like to spend their money on food and good restaurants.

When Iranians go to a restaurant; they prefer to enjoy the food rather than talk about politics, the economy or the weather. The whole conversation turns only around the taste, the color, the flavor and the meal's recipe or the next restaurant.

Persian cuisine usually includes a wide selection of vegetables and herbs. No food is made without onions, garlic, caraway and turmeric, but contrary to some neighboring countries, the amount of spices is lighter in Iranian cuisine.

These preferences are also found in beverages. Iranians like to drink *Dough*; a lightly salted yoghurt drink that's often refined with spices or herbs.

Many years ago, when I was visiting my mother-in-law, she asked me to cook something Persian. I agreed and entered a German kitchen for the first time. Desperately I looked for fresh onions, garlic, herbs and spices, but it was in vain.

I fetched my mother-in-law, and she told me that they never use onions, garlic, or spices. She pointed to a shelf above the stove, in which I could find only salt and pepper. I couldn't make a food without my special spices; at last, I gave up. We ordered food for delivery.

But how do the Germans cook their dishes? In Persian cuisine there is almost no food without these ingredients. With some foods we even eat raw onions – we have different kinds of onions. One in particular, is sweet and tastes just great. My daughter loves raw onions. She always asks for it especially in Chinese restaurants, even to the point where it occasionally embarrasses my husband.

Nowadays in Germany everyone has an extra kitchen cabinet for all exotic spices and herbs. The renowned names of cafés and restaurants from everywhere in the world have branches in each part of the town with a wide variety of foods available.

These are all advantages that come with immigrants' distinctive gastronomy and add to the glamour and glitter of each city. Today the Germans speak foreign languages more often, and they are more interested in foreign cultures and cuisine.

In architecture, immigrant cultural influence is slowly but vividly changing too. Thank God! Buildings now frequently include patios and larger windows.

As a Middle Eastian you suffer if you are to live in a German apartment or house: rooms without closets, small kitchens and bathrooms with drab or muted color, or even without color, without spirit. I have felt closed in by small windows, darkness, no curvatures or stucco on the ceilings. The lack of patios feels depressing and unfriendly.

Even within traditional families, women and the long hours they spend in the kitchen are respected in the Middle East. Kitchens have large windows or access to garden. Many have a door to the outside in order to ventilate steam and odors from inside out. Kitchens are colorful. There are a lot of cabinets in which all kinds of spices, herbs, various kinds of oil and always *Ghee* can be found (solid oil that's used for foods that take longer to cook).

The importance of the kitchen reflects how Persians value food. Food is a part of the culture, and also good food creates good moods. Iranians strongly believe in "A sound mind in a sound body." Living abroad, I have found that food from different cultures can also bring people closer together.

An important peculiarity in the Iranian traditional gastronomy and health is the distinction of foods and drinks in two categories of "warm" and "cold". These terms are not referred to the temperature of the foods or the way they are prepared, but on the assumed effects they have on the body when consumed. The Iranian cooks are always eager to combine warm and cold foods in such a way that they create intermal balance and harmony. The philosophy of Persian cuisine is based on the states which may lead to physical or mental malaise, discomforts and even illnesses. If you eat without balance, for example, it is assumed that depression can come from too much cold food.

Warm foods include bread made from wheat, honey, meat from turkey, duck and lamb, figs, grapes, almonds, honeydew melons, black tea, mustard, basil, dates, peas, beans, chickpeas and eggs.

Cold foods, on the other hand, include malt bread, beef and chicken meat, corn, fish, lettuce, dairy products, rice, zucchini, spinach, mushrooms and almost all kinds of fruit.

In summer, yoghurt and cucumbers, mint, fruits and vegetables are often eaten, and boiled foods are eaten in smaller quantity. This is complemented by lots of tea, because the body cools down from sweating.

In winter, a lot of ginger, saffron tea and healthy meals are on the menu.

Invitation for dinner

If you're visiting Iran, you can be sure you will be invited for dinner with a Persian family. It will be an excellent opportunity to learn something about Persian cuisine, the country and the people. Here are some things you'll want to know before you go.

You'd better know if you are invited to dinner at 8 pm, often guests will show up around 9 pm or even later, but nobody would complain or feel compelled to give an explanation.

It's a good idea to arrive at an invitation neither thirsty nor hungry, not to put a burden on the host from the first moment. When we used to get invited to a party, our mom would have given us some snack before leaving the house. She didn't want us to become impatient in case the mealtime was delayed.

Greeting in Iran is very affectionate and warm; it includes three consecutive kisses between two men or two women. This may sound strange in the western world where kisses on the cheeks are being exchanged between men and women. The custom would seem grotesque, gross and unusual in Germany, but in Iran it's just a sign of true and genuine affection and friendship between men and women.

After the greetings, women routinely rush into the cloakroom in order to lavish themselves in their imposed coats and scarves, freshen up their hair, and apply their facial make-up. After all, we women have invested a lot of effort into looking beautiful. Men like it too, so this is a win-win situation. At an official dinner, T-shirts and jeans are not seen anywhere, except among the youth. Ladies often wear their best and newest clothes. They usually wear excessive amounts of red lipstick. Shirts and jackets are expected for men, sometimes even a suit and tie, depending on their age. Dinnerwear in Tehran is similar to what one would wear to a wedding Germany.

While the ladies are still freshening up, the men have already met each other and started chatting. Usually 15 to 20 people from all ages come to these parties: friends, relatives, parents, siblings, grandma, grandpa, coworkers; old and young, big and small. Dinner hosts aspire to create a very cozy atmosphere that makes everyone feel at home.

In Germany, at a party before the main food, appetizers are usually served. In Iran, tea and pastries are served as the appetizer.

In Germany, fruits are normally found in a bowl in the kitchen or in the lounge, but in Iran fruit is served like a cake in separate dishes for every guest individually. A small plate filled with orange, tangerine, small cucumber, grapes, banana and kiwi etc. is placed before each guest. What the guests are served is seasonal and changes from a variety of fruits to nuts. Pistachios are always included.

If you think it's now about time to have the dinner served, think again! First, the guests are asked to a table with more appetizers, usually served cold. You will find plenty of small, delicious foods on the table made with love. Guests are helping themselves by taking the small bites on the small plates. There are also beverages. If you want some, you take some!

Guests start spirited and loud conversations, while the children are roaming about. Music often plays and there is dancing. On these evenings, Persians enjoy themselves tremendously. Nothing is skimped on and the jocund and jolly host makes the greatest possible effort to be sure that the guests feel well at home.

Frequently I met interesting people at dinner gatherings who readily and honestly offered a short version of their exciting life stories. Often the atmosphere is very cordial, even among those who are meeting for the first time.

Usually, the main dinner is served between 10 and 11pm, and not only is not served one dish as the main course, but also at least four or five dishes are being prepared and served on large trays or in big bowls. Various rices decorated by zaffron, Persian bread and fresh, eye-catching herbs add to the beauty of the table.

Again, guests are asked to the table to help themselves. Due to the large number of guests, it is often not possible that everyone finds a seat at the table. All guests eat their fill, and the main course is the highlight of the host's hospitality. It is tradition that guests admire the host's cooking skill repeatedly and loudly.

There are beverages before and after dinner, but not when the main dishes are on the table. According to the Persian ancient medicine, drinking along with eating is not healthy, because it dilutes the digestive juices and it can lead to health problems. Alcoholic beverages of course are entirely prohibited and punishable by law. One shouldn't ask for them, but they can be found at each home precisely because they are prohibited. Perhaps this is a natural human reaction to everything banned and forbidden.

For years, I've lived in a conservative family in Germany with strict table etiquette and manners. It is the reason why I am puzzled by the fact that Iranians neither abide by the seating and dress codes nor the punctuality. Usually on the table people just sit next to the person they want to have conversation with, except the head of the table which is reserved for the host or hostess. Sometimes I see, to my surprise, six men sitting next to each other. To my wonder, any time I point out to these code violations, nobody listens to me or they say, "Why? We are comfortable. Besides it is cozy."

The dinner is not quite over even when the first guests start to leave and say good bye. The guests who stay longer sit together after dinner and entertain themselves. Each guest feels responsible for the delight of the whole group and therefore they will tell jokes or funny anecdotes.

Men like to talk about young and beautiful women when their wives are busy cleaning the table or attending the kids, in other words, when the women are distracted. Women are the number one topic, followed by soccer, cars, jobs, travel and money, and last but not least, politics.

After dinner, men like to play backgammon. There is a nice history to this game: Hundreds of years ago, an Indian king visiting Persia brought a game of chess along to give to his host, the Shah, or king of Persia. He stated that victory in war always comes with deep thoughts and precise execution. The Persian king wanted to return the favor and to express his gratitude. He gave his guest a board game which didn't need to be played with such seriousness and silence as chess and told him that in order to win you also need luck. The game was supposed to offer a combination of intelligence, luck, joy and fun elements.

Backgammon is a fun game that has been played for thousands of years in Persia. During the game, two players siting face-to-face fire each other up by using expressions and keep bragging and bluffing to discourage each other. It greatly amuses me to watch them playing. It is so exciting, but unbelievable how they can hurl even vulgar and swearwords at each other and simultaneously be so deeply focused to take relentless effort to win by all means, as if they were fighting for their family's' honor.

Finally, leaving the house, the guests express their sincere gratitude. It is customary to say thanks more than once, sometimes you stand in the doorway for half an hour to say goodbye!

Compliments

Persians always like to offer compliments. Beautiful young women are spoiled daily with verses, poetry and metaphors. Even women complement each other. However, the charming compliments from men to women should not be considered as sexual overtures.

The game of attention and compliment will add spice to the routine of the Iranian women's daily life as soon as they leave the house. If these compliments are subtle, creative and cautious, the world of women will take them positively, and even consider them the element of self-acknowledgment, recognition, respect and pride as long as they do not violate the dignity or embarrass them in any way.

Since there are no discos, night clubs or other forms of co-ed entertainment, and the genders are also strictly separated in sports and schools. Young people try to find other opportunities to communicate with each other, for example, in a shopping mall, at a grocery store, in a pharmacy or in a café.

Sometimes, in order to look manlier or attract the women's attention, men pay at the supermarket checkout for the women who appeal to them or ask the women politely to carry their bags. Women might also get a bouquet of flowers when they're shopping. It's only meant as a gesture by men, and they just can't help it. It is nice but it could be interpreted as a little bothersome, a little annoying. My point is that beautiful women are being spoiled by daily small gestures everywhere.

One day, my friend and I were waiting in a long line at a bakery, suddenly my beautiful girlfriend Sepide got fed up and simply cut the line, passed everyone and stood in front. The employees immediately turned to her and asked if they could help her. Nobody complained about her misdeed of not respecting the right of the others or at least reminding her about where her spot in line was. On the contrary, those people were truly mesmerized by her beauty and allowed her to do that.

But on the other hand, you might also experience the opposite. One day, I really wasn't in a good mood and wanted to hang around the mall to cheer myself up. I put on an old coat of my mom's which almost made me look old, took a taxi and went to the shopping center. In front of the store the public-moral-guardians were standing and checking if the women wore makeup or the proper scarves.

Having seen that scene, I asked the taxi driver to drive me back home. He looked into the rearview mirror and asked: "Why? "

"Because of the guardians, I don't want to get into any trouble. " I answered.

He looked at me again through the mirror "Just go there and do your shopping I can guarantee they won't bother you, hundred percent sure. They are only causing trouble to young and beautiful women," he answered.

I got off the car and with a smile told him: "Thanks for the compliment."

A few years ago, Sepide came to Germany; her parents wanted her to continue her studies there.

She stayed in Düsseldorf for three months, and thereafter she decided to return back to Tehran. When I asked her the reason, she said: "I feel lonely and isolated here in Germany. I'm unwillingly confined into my own cocoon. There is no actual warmth and sympathy among people here. Nobody cares about me or even notices me. Everyone is busy and caring about himself. Everything is too serious, correct and impersonal; it is too cold and spiritless for me. "

She missed the attention lavished on beautiful women in Iran, the smiles, the compliments, and the friendliness in dealing with each other in daily life, the encouraging and motivating words. She missed her home.

Beauty, health and well-being

Persia is the country of Naturopathy. In a lot of small villages there are no hospitals, but instead, the elderly people share a lot of traditional prescriptions.

Iranians now take a lot of pills before, during and after meals, including natural remedies. The reason behind this eagerness might be traced back to the ancient times.

When I inform them about harmful and detrimental side effects of the drugs, they try to convince me by such a flimsy and untenable remark "Do you know that this medication has been prescribed by *the* Professor so and so of the university of so and so? He's got a six months waiting list."

Pharmacies in Iran are true gold mines, and they are always crowded. Iranians like to take medications and most of all; they trust western-made pharmaceutical drugs.

Natural healing methods are also increasingly valued. All of my brothers are physicians, but whenever we were at my mother's home and somebody falls ill, she will fetch her natural medicine right away even if the patient is one of my brothers.

In these cases she repeatedly told them, "You have no idea, I raised seven kids with these medicine exclusively. If I was supposed to wait for doctors every time, or for your father to go to the pharmacy, who knows what would have happened to you! "

My aunt for example suffers from high blood pressure. Once we were en route outside of Tehran and she became so upset that her blood pressure rose severely. She got headache and nosebleed at the same time, and then she panicked, because she didn't have her medicine on her. My mom brought a bowl of lukewarm water, grated a few garlic cloves and poured into the water. Then she asked my aunt to place her feet into the bowl. In a few minutes my aunt felt well again.

We have good natural remedies in Iran, many of which still are surely unheard of in the West.

I am an alternative medicine practitioner with a daughter of 25 years. I am not young anymore, but every time I talk on the phone to my mom who lives in the USA, she anxiously asks me whether I got a permanent job at the hospital.

What am I supposed to say to my mom? Should I tell her that still we have not reached the time where alternative medicine practitioners and doctors work alongside each other in the hospitals letting patients choose the treatment method of their own choice? That alternative medicine isn't equal yet? That I am too old to get employed? No matter how old you are, you'll always remain a naïve kid in the eyes of your parents.

Iranians are always eager to be fit and beautiful. Women especially are under enormous pressure to look always beautiful and young, even if they are older and have grown-up children. This is certainly the reason why esthetic surgery is booming in Iran.

In Tehran alone, there are some 3,000 plastic surgeons according to reports. Iranians seem to be particularly unhappy about their noses: it is estimated that at least 70,000 nose jobs are performed annually in Iran. When women with an affluent background meet each other, the latest plastic surgeries they have had are often the conversation topic.

I realized it when I read an online ad, that the "beauty mania" can become really dangerous. According to that ad, a young Persian woman offered her kidney in order to be able to finance a cosmetic surgery. Others fall victim to a diet mania that can also become perilous.

I have a relative in Tehran; she is 70 years old and suffers from Parkinson disease. When I visited her and asked how I could be of any assistance or do her a favor, she answered, "I want to look better and younger. Would you dye my hair and eyebrows blonde? That would make me so happy." Because of her illness, she could barely walk; she was practically bedbound, but she wished to look better. Well, I took her wish seriously and dyed her white hair and eyebrows. Her joy was beyond imagination.

In Tehran particularly, people aren't merely concerned about beauty, but also about well-being, as a balance to the stressful urban life. Women, the older ones specially, enjoy yoga and meditations.

In general, the Persians are open-minded towards everything that addresses the sixth sense. You can find offerings for hypnosis, meditation, fortune-telling or dream interpretation everywhere, but unfortunately, superstition is also wide-spread, and it is easily seen in daily life. For example, if you put off your shoes and they fall atop of one another, then a journey is supposed to be just around the corner.

It is believed that, having a pet can shield humans from evil and vicious energies. When a home pet dies, it is assumed that the pet has taken away the bad energies and protected its owner from all negativities by its death.

Neighbors

On my last trip, my brother and his wife had planned an excursion for me. A three-day trip to a very beautiful and ancient town called "Kashan".

There are many beautiful cities in Iran. To visit them all, you'll need at least six months. The cities and regions differ by their climate, architecture and history. When it is freezing cold and snowing in Caspian Sea area in the North, one could play golf or go swimming in Persian Gulf in the South. There are also major differences in regard to the traditions, languages and dialects. Iran is a multiethnic country. Apart from Farsi, the official language, there are also Kurdish, Turkish, Luri, Baluchi, Arabic, Armenian and a lot of other languages and dialects. Depending on which ethnic background they belong to, Iranians also differ in term of their appearances.

People in the North, near the Russian border often have blue, green or honey brown colored eyes and a lighter skin. They are also usually very smart. It is claimed that, the reason behind it is enjoying good climate with clean coastal air and the excessive consumption of fresh fish, fish oil, mountain herbs and vegetables daily for generations. Many famous doctors, scientists, authors and painters hailed from this region.

The people in the Southern region around Persian Gulf have rather dark eyes and skin-color with curly hair.

Before leaving the house, my sister-in-law visited her neighbor with a bouquet of flowers. Seemingly, she had already given her the spare keys to the house, so that the neighbor could take care of the plants and the house in our absence. So much confidence evoked my admiration and respect; I was speechless for a moment for such a mutual trust.

In Iran, people always respect their neighbors; actually neighbors in Iran are best friends and confidants who are consulted in many matters. After all, you live door to door with them, you meet them all the time and you can rely on them in so many ways, for example receiving the mail or packages, mutually taking care of the plants or pets and so on. When someone is sick and alone, neighbors come over and help out. Neighbors cook for one another, do grocery shopping and even pick up the kids from school. That's priceless, and something that is hardly seen in Germany. As long as the neighbors are treated well and respectfully, they are like family. It is nicer to get along well with the neighbors than to ignore them. I think the harmonious and peaceful coexistence can make everyone involved stronger and more humane.

Kashan:

The city is located some 200 kilometers south of Tehran at the northern edge of the Kuhrud Mountains on the fringes of the central Iranian desert. The city is surrounded by the first large oasis along the road leading from Qom to Kerman.

In 1778, the city was almost completely by an earthquake. The subsequent reconstruction of the town during the Qajar dynasty with its spacious structures today is a tourist attraction.

This includes the Agha Bozorg Mosque.

Kashan is also known for the Fin Garden covering 2.3 hectares (also known as Bāgh-e Fin). It contains architectural elements from the Safavid, Zand and Qajar periods.

With its numerous fountains, water pools, water runs and old trees; it belongs to the most famous and most beautiful gardens in Iran. In the western sections of the garden, the Kashan National Museum with many archeological discoveries is located. It also contains ethnographic exhibits and calligraphies made by Qajar period artists.

Fin Garden received a sad kind of popularity by Amir Kabir (also known as Mirza Taghi Chan). The Prime Minister, a reformer of his times with whose name ideas of diplomacy and cleverness are connected to this day, was ostracized to these gardens in 1851 by the king and he was murdered in 1852, allegedly by envoys of the king.

Historic Tabatabei House, Kashan

Bāgh-e Fin Garden, Kaschan

Shiraz – city of poetry

The city is located some 700 kilometers south of Tehran in the southern part of the Zagros Mountains at an elevation of about 1500 meters above sea level. Shiraz and the region have been the center of Achaemenid Persia more than 2,500 years ago.

Two powerful old-Persian royal houses are from here: the ancient Achaemenids (559-330 B.C.) and the Sasanians (224-651). In the octagonal pavilion of the Pars Museum, visitors can learn all about the region and its dynasties.

Shiraz is often referred to as the „Garden of Iran", as the city features an omnipresent wealth of flowers, particularly the famous rose varieties.

In Shiraz, two of Persia's best-known poets – Hafez and Saadi – are buried in mausoleums. The mausoleums today are pilgrimage sites for writers and tourist attractions at the same time.

Shiraz has gained an abstract famousness through the varietal if the same name – as the consumption of alcohol has been prohibited since 1979; this only remains a historic reminiscence.

Mausoleum of Hafez, Shiraz

Persepolis – the pride of ancient Persia

The old Persian royal seat city of Persepolis (*Tacht-e Dschamschid* „throne of Jamshid") was one of the capitals of ancient Persia under the Achaemenids and was founded in 520 B.C. by Dareios I. in the Persis region of southern Iran.

The name „Persepolis" derives from the Greek language and means „city of Persians"; the Persian name refers to Jamshid, an ancient king.

When the former royal seat Pasargadae was moved here from 50 kilometers away, a terrace covering 15 hectares was prepared at the foot of the mountain *Kuh-e Mehr (*also called *Kuh-e Rahmat*). More than 14 buildings have been constructed on the platform under Darius I. and his successors, including Xerxes, Artaxerxes I. and Artaxerxes II. Further palaces have been excavated at the foot of the terrace.

The palace town was destroyed by arson in 330 B.C. by Alexander the Great, but its (partly reconstructed) remains can still be viewed today.

It is today known that the fire ironically has caused something good – some 30,000 clay tablets were hardened by the heat to such a degree that they can tell the history of the city to archeologists more than 2,000 years later in great detail.

Persepolis is a UNESCO world heritage site and is located some 60 kilometers northeast of Shiraz on the Marvdasht plateau.

Persepolis

Stroke of fate

Our neighbor's brother, who comes from a very nice family, got married to a very beautiful girl. That called for a grand and awesome celebration for the happy couple who lived near Tehran.

After a while, the newlywed couple decided to move to Tehran because the girl was pregnant and the medical care in Tehran was better in all aspects than in their village.

They rented an apartment not far from his brother. The groom had two brothers, one was married already and lived on our street and the other was single. Both brothers helped him with pleasure when he moved to Tehran. On the last day of the moving, Sasan, the groom, said that he didn't need any help anymore and he could take care of the rest alone. His wife Darya (the name means "sea") was an expectant mother. She was deliriously happy and overjoyed: a new town, a new apartment and a baby soon. Everything seemed to be just perfect for the couple.

Sasan loaded the rest of the furniture into his car and drove to Tehran. Very close to the city something terrible happened. A truck driver did not pay attention to the right of the road and collided with Sasan's car with full impact, Sasan died on the spot at the prime of his life. His wife was seven months pregnant at the time of accident. It was a huge tragedy, a sad and unfair tragedy.

The situation was unbearable for several days. There was only grief, sorrow, anguish and despair. A few days after the tragedy, the bereaved family deliberated and discussed possible remedies for the unexpected loss. It was a Rubicon in their lives. After a while, they decided based on Persian tradition that Sasan's younger brother "Sina" marry his deceased brother's widow in a private family gathering in order to prevent further family tragedy. Sina accepted to patronize emotionally and financially the unborn baby. They didn't want the baby to step into this world as an orphan child.

The family didn't want to allow a young widow grieving over the loss of her beloved husband and the dolorous fate of her unborn baby to also deal with uncertainty. They wanted to conceal the bitter truth of the untimely death of the father from the child in the future as well; so they prearranged everything in all secrecy.

Shortly after the funeral, Darya and Sina got married. They had a common pain and sorrow. Together, they could seethe and soothe with that fathomless sorrow, they could try to heal their wounds, and to console each other. They hoped to find affection for one another in the course of time. Finally a healthy and wonderful boy was born. Everyone was infinitely happy again.

A short time later, the newly married couple moved away from the district. They wanted to shield the family against any gossip and rumor. They didn't want the child to be informed in the future about the sad story and the loss of his biological father by the neighbors.

Dogs

It is about time to change the way of thinking. In Iran there are many stray dogs. Dogs, just like pigs, are considered impure and not clean to be touched in Islamic tradition, although police do use German shepherds to track down illicit drugs. In my opinion, it doesn't fit to our modern times that the stray dogs go without any guardians or without any kind of medical attention and eat musty and moldy food they find to survive. I believe these views are a thing of the past and people should rethink how they treat dogs.

Some relatives of mine who are living north of Tehran in a district across from some beautiful hills very discreetly look after the stray dogs living on one of those hills of the neighborhood. They built a doghouse and even put a Persian rug in it. They take care of the food, the medical care and other necessities of the dogs to save them. The neighbors have provided the dogs with those facilities; otherwise the city municipality has threatened to euthanize the dogs.

The dogs' gratitude was noticeable.

Every time that the neighbors brought food, the dogs looked into their eyes for minutes prior to start to eat the food, and in the night they barked as a token of their thankfulness, as if they wanted to say "You sleep peacefully, we will be up for you to watch over your homes in the night".

The presence of the dogs had brought fervor and happiness to the whole neighborhood. They were like a palladium for all the neighbors. But the dogs were a thorn in the eyes of old, bitter, medieval-thinking Mrs. Bahram.

One day the female dog that had to take care of four puppies was run over by a car. The poor dog's hind legs were broken in the accident. Her death, and that of her puppies, seemed imminent.

A caring neighbor brought the poor dog to a veterinary clinic, but the people in charge were going to help the animals only if they were paid in advance. She called another neighbor to share the costs because she couldn't afford the surgery on her own.

The dog received surgery and could return to her puppies with a cast. The gratitude of the dogs was palpable. They were barking again in the night.

That sign of faithfulness and the protective manner of the dogs were interpreted wrongly by the mean and malicious female neighbor. She felt bothered and annoyed by the barking, so she alarmed the authorities. They came at night without warning, drugged the dogs to avoid a certain protest and commotion by the neighborhood, and removed the dogs. They also took away the female dog and her puppies.

The next morning, when the neighbors woke up, they were shocked and heartbroken by the absence of the dogs. They searched the entire area then started to talk on the phone with the authorities. They didn't want to accept that something terrible might have happened to the poor dogs; namely euthanasia. Until this day, the dogs have remained missing. One can really imagine those dog's fates!

What followed next was one of the most dramatic scenes I've ever experienced in my life. The male dog returned and retreated to the top of the hill while looking for his missing family. It didn't reside in the doghouse anymore. He just kept wandering sadly on the hill and yearningly awaiting his family to return.

Another time I was sitting in a share taxi, the driver was waiting for more passengers to fill the car. Next to me was an elderly lady sitting with a bag on her lap. She had her hands on the bag and kept caressing it all the time.

The driver watched it all through the rearview mirror and all of a sudden, he yelled at the woman and frantically asked her if she had a dog in that bag.

The woman said: "Yes, but a very small and very well trained one. "

The taxi driver asked her to get off.

I told the driver, "We could go as a private ride. I will pay the costs and please take the lady where she wants to go. "

The taxi driver replied, "And what if I get into a checking-control? Then I'll have to pay an expensive fine for that." Again, he asked her to get off.

She got off, but it was not humiliating enough for the old lady with the dog. The taxi driver got off the car too and yelled angrily over to his colleagues who were waiting for passengers, "That woman's got a dog in her bag! "

I got off the taxi too, wiping away my tears and thought, "Why can't some of us behave a little more kindly and humanly and treat each other in a friendly manner? Why?"

Tehran's Mother Theresa

When I was in Tehran a few weeks ago, some relatives told me about an extraordinarily loving, humanistic, social-minded woman who had been attending orphans and people in dire need for decades. Her name was Maryam and everyone called her "Mother". I was eager to meet her.

I had an intuition that the encounter with this reverent woman will be a special experience. So, after contacting her we set up a meeting. A small delicate woman full of energy and a charisma awaited me. She talked to me about her life and her sufferings.

For herself she expects nothing. Everything she gets from donations goes to the people in dire straits to help them to survive and cope. Her house is always open to the deprived and the needy. She doesn't even lock the door. There is a sign at the door that reminds people to take off their shoes when entering, even if she is not at home.

She gets donations from sympathetic and humanitarian individuals. Unfortunately, in Iran, taking care of the old, sick, and the needy falls upon families. In fact, it is the family that provides someone with welfare. There is neither social security authority nor public welfare. The street children, people who don't have a family, women who have been divorced or run away from an abusive family or husband and have no income, the old and sick people and the other social outcasts have nothing. No family means any help or support.

Providing support is being executed by charitable people like the Mother Theresa of Tehran. She has dedicated her life to people in need, regardless of their age, young or old. She provides them with meals, accommodations, and medicine as best she can. Among her numerous philanthropic endeavors she even takes care of these destitute peoples' birthdays by sending them good wishes for the New Year. She tries to put a ray of hope into their hearts.

In all that, she is entirely dedicated to them. She did not settle down to start a family just in order to be able to be there for people in need.

What touched me in particular after the long face-to-face conversation we had was her generosity in giving me the only jewelry she was wearing. As a symbol of our new friendship, she gave me a ring with semiprecious Iranian turquoise *(firouze)*. She said it symbolized our dedication to humane causes that connected us despite the long distance, and as a source of perseverance in case of facing problems in life. With her gift, I could always be reminded that there are people with much bigger problems who are waiting for our helping hand. There are so few people who have such a big heart and altruistic mind. She has dedicated her life to service for the good of others, and is an inspiring example for all of us.

What she has been given back from this life of dedication is the solemn conviction to do the right thing. She thanks God for the boon and the opportunity of meeting all those helpless people. And that is what makes this amazing woman radiate like a saint. With her almost 60 years, she looks 20 years younger and she has an aura that fascinates everyone.

Today, I am still in contact with her from Germany and sometimes when she has a special project, I support her and her organization as much as I can.

Golf

One day, I wanted to check out a golf course in Tehran, so I drove to the city's most beautiful golf club.

I entered the registration room and asked for a golf trainer. I was told that only a female coach had permission to train me. I accepted that, paid and went to the golf course with my coach. While we were playing, she repeated proudly again and again about her fame, the number of overseas tournaments she had participated in, and her popularity.

A few days later, when I was back at the golf course again, I was informed that the designated trainer had unfortunately left the country, and they had no substitute available. I sat at the golf course, tense and puzzled, and wondered what to do next.

After a few minutes, a young man whom I had seen in the golf club walked up to me and told me that he had learned that the women were allowed to receive lessons from male coaches too. I couldn't believe it. "Wow! What great news!" I thought. Naively I believed him. I paid and we entered the playing field. In a flash, he gave me a few tips then said he had to leave me for a moment and asked me to continue practicing.

After half an hour he returned, gave more advice, and then left me again for a few minutes. This was so odd to me; something that would never happen in Germany. I was confused. He did not return a second time and I finally returned home.

When I called the golf club the next day to book a trainer they told me, "Male trainers cannot teach women and it has been this way for years now." I finally realized why he kept leaving me on my own. Trainers often don't have a busy schedule throughout the day. So, how can they financially support their lives, how can they get by and subsist on a pittance income? They want to look good, they want to throw parties, pamper their girlfriends. He must have wanted to make a little extra money so he trained me, but he couldn't get caught.

Wrestlers

For the last two thousand years, the national sport in Persia has been wrestling, or *Koshti*. Renowned Iranian epic poet Ferdowsi has written about wrestler heroes *"Pahlavan"* and their heroic deeds; the book of the Kings "Shahnameh"has made wrestling even more popular.

Wrestling is an entirely male style of fighting in Iran. Wrestlers are a disciplined and traditional type of masculine; the type of man whose words have value, and who keep their promises. These men were the epitome of chivalry and bravery and have always shown greatness in their readiness to stand up for the rights of the people. These strong men provide a sense of safety for women.

I like wrestlers and I have a lot of respect for them. They aren't merely athletes but humanitarians who act humanely. I can't find the right words to describe their characteristics and their altruistic souls as they really are just heroes or "Pahlevans".

I remember well, whenever I wanted to entertain my younger brothers, I would often spread a large blanket on the floor and let my brothers wrestle. Father or my cousins were the referees and spectators and knew a lot more about *Koshti* than I did.

My father loved *Koshti*; he knew the rules well and gave advice to both of my brothers at the same time. My brothers liked to wrestle and we were all having fun. One wins this game if he pushes his opponent's shoulder to the ground, then the fight is over.

Actually, these benevolent and genuine heroes who display heroic deeds are committed to social causes. In their surroundings, nobody shall suffer or live in dire need. They take care of any problem in their neighborhoods. From the remote past until today such Heroes in every part of town make people feel safe and secure. Widows, orphans, poor people, or those who needed protection or advice could always count on these wrestler heroes. Wrestlers are still well-respected in Iran. One can compare their nature with Robin Hood and maybe his story was inspired by the wrestlers.

The most famous and popular Iranian wrestler and Olympian of all times was and still is Takhti, an extraordinary man, a true hero, a protector who was loved and followed by many. His pictures or portraits can still be seen on the walls of many shops, especially in southern Tehran where he had grown up. There is even an international stadium named after him, just as a sign of paying everlasting homage and tribute to him. If you want to look favor in the eyes of the old generation, you should know the name: Takhti "Jahan Pahlavan" "Hero of the world".

Wrestlers (Koshtigir) were not always welcome with everyone. Many years ago, during the turmoil of the nationalization of Iranian Oil Company under Prime

Minister Mossadegh, Takhti who was on the peak of his success and popularity, in the prime of his life, mysteriously committed suicide.

Many people believe he was assassinated for his political ideas, and the danger he posed to the government at that time.

Women and Sports

Traditionally in Iran, women prefer to watch sports rather than participate in them. Sports are watched with enthusiasm, but not taken too seriously. Persian women are homey rather than outgoing and active. You can often hear "Take it easy, one shouldn't overdo it. "If they do sports, they just dabble.

The number of gyms in which women can exercise is small outside of Tehran and other metropolitan cities, and the choice of classes is meager.

One day, when I was walking along a street, a flyer fell into my hands. It was about the opening of a gym for women but oddly, the image on the flyer was a muscular man in a short, tight top. I burst into laughter. It was just so funny. Lawfully, photos of women on ads are forbidden, unless they are wearing headscarves. Since sport advertising with headscarf looks rather ridiculous and unathletic, it is rarely seen.

I have been in different gyms a few times and I made some astounding observations there. First of all, unlike women in Germany, Persian women are not punctual and miss the first few minutes of classes. They also favor their make up to sweating so they don't move vigorously. They want to leave looking as nice as when they arrived. Most of them consider signing up for the gym and buying matching sports garments half as much athletic achievement as actually doing sport.

When the trainer starts the class, the complaints and grumbling are heard from every corner:

"Not yet please! "

"What? Why so fast? "

"It's warm here. It is stuffy in here! "

A few minutes before the class is over, they stop again, but at least they have a good conscience that they have been at the gym!

When they get back home, they have to lie down for hours. "One shouldn't overdo it. One needs to rest a bit first."

So, fitness isn't top on the list for women in Iran. In particular, women of the younger generation love dancing. It is not the classic dances, but just a special type of dancing without complicated steps. As a matter of fact, they take a series of steps in rhythm and in tune to Persian, Turkish or Arabian music. The women move back and forth to the music and they feel to be on the cloud nine when dancing.

As a little girl, I was rather tall compared to my peers. As the sister of four boys, I always had to play soccer with them, as the goalkeeper. I feel pity for goalkeepers, because I remember having to make a decision in fractions of a second, either for my nose and beauty or for my team and victory every time the ball came back flying at me with full force. Every time and without exception, I had decided in favor of my nose. Thanks for that, but I was often scolded, "You are so tall but practically useless as a goalkeeper. Which team you are playing for? Don't you have any sympathy for your team? Are you blind? "

But I couldn't help it. It was my own fixed rule: The ball shouldn't hit the face. Everything else was allowed. How often I had my fingers broken during the games and I kept on playing anyway. Even today, two of my fingers are bent because they have been healed on their own without medical care at the time. These fingers remind me of my happy childhood.

Sometimes when I couldn't play because of injuries, I assumed the referee role. I have to confess the truth that I couldn't make any decisions without bias.

Soccer is very popular in Iran. By now, there are even women teams playing that game in front of the male crowd. When they play, they wear scarves and long pants, so that only their faces and hands are not covered.

Persians have good taste and a fondness for chic and elegant sports, where these are rather seen as relaxation, entertainment or for releasing stress, not as a hard training which takes perseverance and hard work. Persian women like horseback riding, golf or archery, because it looks so ritzy.

An acquaintance who owned horses once took me along to his riding club on the outskirts of the city.

Similar to Germany, it was conspicuous that Equestrian sport was more a women's domain. The young girls and women were rouged and coiffed beyond a reasonable degree. The designs of their clothes were so trendy that nobody could guess they were at the horse stable! In Germany, horse owners or even horseback riders take care of their horses almost every day, including brushing the fur, cleaning the horseshoes, saddling the horse and everything else. The horse owner, rather than the rider, takes care of all of these things.

To my wonder, all of these tasks were done by my acquaintance at his riding club, and his wife just needed to mount on the horse and start riding. Seeing this, I realized how the ladies' outfits could look like new.

The largest sport club in Tehran is as large as a village and is called *Bashgahe Enghelab*, or Enghelab Stadium. The stadium serves so many sport lovers with services in tennis, golf, archery, squash, bowling, gyms and other kinds of sport. A long and beautiful path lined by trees that arch gracefully over the walkway invites many sport fans every day for jogging, walking or just strolling.

You can see a lot of people exercising in the mornings or on weekdays and many more sitting at the club's café along the jogging path, drinking something and talking.

Many beautiful women and men of all ages visit the stadium, whether pursuing athletic activities or just enjoying their pastimes. Surprisingly, the number of women seems to be increasing. One thing that most of the women and the young girls have in common is the effort they put in to perfecting their outfits. Sunglasses in particular are a status symbol at the stadium.

Bashgahe Enghelab is actually only open to the members, but you can purchase a day ticket to use the facilities. I like using this opportunity when I am in Tehran. The beautiful path invites you for a walk, and afterwards, I like to sit in the café and drink something. During my few days in Tehran, I am not particularly keen on exercising, but rather looking for relaxation. I simply enjoy watching people. Many other visitors of this sport club do the same.

Beauty salons for the soul

Beauty salons, particularly hairdressing salons in Tehran, are stories in themselves. Spending time in these places lifts the spirit tremendously. They are pure antidepressants!

I make my appointment from Germany even before I arrive in Theran. Salons are always well booked, but beyond the practical reason for booking early, I am addicted to the atmosphere I find there and don't want to miss it when I visit.

Everything is situated in separate large and colorful rooms, each with a homely ambience: hairdressing, facial beauty, epilation, manicure and pedicure.

There are often foreign-made cosmetics for sale, great clothes, shoes and accessories such as costumes, jewelry and scarves. In addition to the salon and the retail shopping, you get a free life advice or marriage counseling on the side.

Unfortunately, there are also tips on health or illness issues, on various diets that will tell you how to lose weight easily and fast. Tips on losing weight are in high demand and the dietary supplements are sold as well. If you complain about the stomach pain or the headache you will immediately get advices from different people regarding what remedies might help. You can find medications to stabalize circulation, flatulence, insomnia or tranquilization. I always have the impression that they carry a small pharmacy around with them.

Actually, the contents of an Iranian woman's purse differ a lot from those of a German woman's. Persians often carry a lot of cosmetics, tranquilizers, pain remedies such as Aspirin and other drugs. In addition, women carry many pieces of paper in the purse listing recommendations where to get foreign clothes, jewelry, scarves and so on.

Medications are taken based on recommendations without asking whether they could have side effects or not. Furthermore, the keys of some neighbors ring clatter in the purse reminding them of checking the houses and watering the plants in the absence of those neighbors, and last but not least, some candies.

The nonstop loud and energetic music permeates the entire space of the parlor. There is always a large Samovar at hand to make fresh tea, as well as biscuits, fruit and nuts. If you're hungry, you'll have a warm lunch delivered to the salon. Nothing is beyond reach for the customer's desires. The boss and her employees are extremely friendly and cheerful, despite their arduous jobs. When they talk to their customers, they address them with nice-sounding denotations, "My darling, my dear, and my beautiful". I don't feel uncomfortable with these intimacies; on the contrary, they make me feel good.

Should I feel the need my future to be read by a fortune teller, one phone call is sufficient. At once, someone will come by and read the cards or the tea leaves. Every wish will be fulfilled. I find a lot of fun in that, it doesn't cost much and there is always a chance that what a fortuneteller says will come true.

I am not superstitious, but I remember the previsions made by a beggar who came to us when I was a child. She was hungry, shabby and sloppily dressed. My mother offered her some food, gave her clothes and some money. She thanked my mother and said, "I would like to compensate your kindness by reading the future on your daughter's palms." When she took a look at my hand, she told me, "You will leave your homeland when you grow up and you'll get married abroad." With a smile on her face, she added that my future husband would be blue-eyed. By that, she meant to say my husband would most likely not be a Persian. Also she noted that my pictures would appear in various foreign newspapers. Filled with fantasy and imagination about the future, we thanked her and said goodbye. Well, what should I say? Many years later, I left my country as a young woman although I loved my country. I married a blue-eyed German and since I worked for UNESCO for a while, there were often pictures of mine in German newspapers and magazines.

Persians have an ancient culture and tradition rooted in mysteries and tales of the past. Still I'm wondering if it was a prediction, a foreshadowing or the beggar's seventh sense.

Access to the beauty salons is strictly forbidden for men. The windows are covered by thick curtains so that noone can see inside the salons. When husbands want to pick up their wives or a taxi driver has to deliver something to a salon, they have to wait in front of the entrance door.

As soon as a woman enters a parlor, she lets her Hijab drop. Persian women are so beautiful and always well dressed. In the beauty salons they feel free. I always marvel about the joie de vivre they radiate, how they laugh and talk without inhibition about their husbands or mothers-in-law. The young girls talk about love and get advices from the older customers who they don't even know. Their voices are soft, they are very feminine and they make delicate gestures when talking. They have charm and radiate eroticism.

It's no wonder that women look quite different when they leave the parlor: new hair color, a new haircut, and a new hairstyle. Women easily make changes. "It's good for a couple not to look the same all the time. Changes preserve the marriage," they say. The hairdressers are really gifted, talented and tasteful.

I feel right at home at any beauty parlor in Tehran. You can simply walk into the kitchen and order something. Even my most extraordinary demands will be met. With a private taxi, everything is possible. The driver takes you anywhere or delivers anything for you. Taxi drivers really have a great place among my favorites in Tehran culture.

In a parlor, you may also be spontaneously invited for a delicious lunch if someone likes you. Isn't that wonderful?

After visiting the parlors not only do you leave with a beautiful and attractive appearance, but you also feel abundantly energetic.

I enjoy the beauty salons in Tehran and I amuse myself by them. Those hours mean a lot to me. To my view, spending time with these jolly people is worth more than a trip or taking one week vacation at the beach.

Lingerie

Tehran is an alluring, lively, and vibrant city, full of contrasts.

One day, when I was window-shopping in a large shopping center, a store with its plain and vacant display window grabbed my attention. It seemed strange and mysterious that there was nothing in its display window, not even a decoration. I passed by the store twice, intentionally, to try to figure out what kind of merchandise was inside. Then surprisingly, I saw a small notice that stated, "Lingerie - No Entrance for Men". Although I had no need for such things, out of curiosity, I decided to step in.

I was as a passionate tourist in my homeland yearning to quench my insatiable curiosity for everything, things that I had missed for years.

When finally I found myself inside the store, ironically enough, I came across the mannequins covered from head to toe according to Islamic woman-dress code. I was truly shocked. "What is this?" I asked myself.

"Hijab" was mandatory and imposed on women, but on the Mannequins inside a place in which the entrance for men was forbidden? It seemed funny. I burst into laughter, but of course stealthily and silently. Then, I noticed the saleswoman was looking at me with a benign smile on her face. Definitely, she couldn't figure out the reason of my wonder. The store had no decoration but the mannequins cloaked in pajamas along with headscarves. Seemingly these mannequins were considered as women, therefore physical protrusions of any body parts (breasts and hip) were not allowed in order to avoid men from any sexual temptation. In Islam, the body of woman is denied. The sight of her breast, in which the sap of life resides, even glimpsed through clothing, is an unforgiveable sin.

Later on, I heard that in all Lingerie stores the front door must be always closed. When you step into the store, you first have to pass through a thick curtain. The reason behind that is preventing men readily from peering into when women open the door. So clever! Once women are finally inside the store, they can take off their coats and headscarves. They are offered beverages and can relax. Once they have the chance to look around, they see what the store has to offer: the finest and most luxurious undergarments, silk stockings in every color, slippers, pajamas and nightgowns.

At last, I picked out a nightgown and took it to the cashier, immersed in my thoughts; all of a sudden a man stepped in hastily. I couldn't believe my eyes. What a brave man! He looked restless and agitated. The shopkeeper starred at him with a look of fear and panic. The man apologized and asked desperately for our help. Aha Moment! It was when the saleswoman overcame her fear, turned her head towards me, "Do you mind if he stay? Otherwise, I can ask him to leave!" "No, no. It's okay." I said bashfully.

The man explained the reason of his entrance. The next day was to be Valentine's Day and he wanted to buy an exquisite and luxurious gift for his wife. He asked the shopkeeper politely to pick out a lovely cloth in size 36 for his wife and promised her to stand aside without touching anything. He was aware of the consequence of his act that most likely would be considered a felony. Presumably, he had put the business license of the store in jeopardy with his entering. The saleswoman quickly found some suitable lingerie in hot pink for him. The man thanked her, paid and hastily left the store. He didn't even wait for his change. His true love to his wife was admirable, and I was thinking what I saw could not be fair. After all, men should really be the ones who pick out and buy expensive lingerie for their wives. Most of the women are way too thrifty when it comes to paying 200 euros for a bra just because it's beautiful, especially if they have children. Instead, they have to constantly think about how they could spend the money on their children.

I left the store and thanked God for not living in this city. Although its contrasts have made it lively, I missed Frankfurt!

In shop windows, female mannequins wear scarves, too

Luxury

In Tehran I feel the true meaning of pure luxury. Middle Eastern architecture is luxurious; from the dazzling kaleidoscope of colorful building facades to ornamental columns, from the wood carvings in door and window frames and wonderful marble floors, to perfectly equipped and spacious kitchens. Bathrooms with colorful and hand-painted tiles, magnificent mosaics, and fireplaces made from marble with fine mosaics fill the senses. Ornaments are omnipresent. They can be found on fabrics, carpets, buildings, wallpapers and decorative art, including hand craftworks. They can be as a singular adornment or basically a part of decoration on the columns, in the stucco of the ceilings, or at building entrances.

Luxury is also found in many residential buildings. There are a lot of tastefully decorated residences with gorgeous silken carpets and curtains, wonderful crystal chandeliers, very fine porcelain and chinaware. Women wear expensive jewelry and the smells of opulent Persian foods such as saffron rice, pistachios and other nuts permeate houses. When served, they are accompanied by an enormous choice of fruit, herbs and vegetables, aromatic saffron tea and a wide selection of fresh bread and caviar, of course.

There is an entirely different atmosphere compared to the residential buildings in Germany in which there is little aroma. When I can smell something, it's the odor of offices; cold and lifeless, void of domestic ambience and spirit kind of without flair, not the warm and rich smells of domestic life in Tehran.

Germans work a lot, often on the weekends as well, so their daily life does not include time for pampering and indulging themselves.

When I had the pleasure to meet the Dalai Lama at one of my UNESCO events, he told me, "You should always attempt to create a lovely atmosphere and ambiance by laying beautiful furniture, colorful objects, flowers, candles, and books, no matter how small the room might be. A beautiful home prolongs longevity and it is also good for the soul."

But Germans prefer to spend their money on vacations and expensive cars. Sometimes, their cars are more valuable than the entirety of furniture in their homes.

Persians live and enjoy what they have and earn. Saving is the last thing on their minds. They throw parties whenever they can for the least and slightest reasons. On the weekend, they always fill their homes with family, friends or neighbors.

Persian houses gleam in many colors, by virtue of their carpets alone, which are mesmerizing; warm and colorful like life itself. You can smell the life and family like jasmine and feel like you are touched. The very feeling gives you the sense of being alive.

I don't think that luxury should be just measured by things you own. Luxury also means taking time for others, and for yourself to enjoy the life and to be open to what the life has to offer you, even if it comes unexpectedly. It means to seize the moment and not always do everything according to plan. To live a luxurious life, you have to seize the moment.

Women and gifts

It is customary in almost every culture that men offer gifts to the woman whom he feels attracted to in order to impress or seduce her. Indeed, in Iran it is the women who have refined the art of receiving gifts more than anywhere else.

I truly believe that Iranian women have come up with this tradition first. History of offering gifts to a loved one as a symbol of respect, sympathy and love goes back to the story of the three Kings' gift offering to Jesus. As we know now, they were Persian Magi from Babylonia. Obviously, they were trained well by their wives or mistresses.

Usually after the first "rendez vous", women are supposed to receive a beautiful present and for each subsequent date as well. However, you should not think that a bouquet of flowers, a box of chocolates and a romantic dinner or something equally cliché will do the trick. No, in addition to that, there have to be expensive perfume, genuine jewelry or similarly valuable presents.

Once, I was eyewitness to a young man getting caught for shop lifting in our neighborhood. As police was taking him away, he started crying loudly and told everybody that he was in love with a girl. He begged people to understand that he needed desperately a present to give her. He didn't want to disappoint or even lose her girlfriend.

The gift-giving doesn't end if a man wants to win the heart of his dream woman. For the engagement only genuine jewelry is allowed and the wedding tops it all. Everything has to be of the finest quality. Otherwise, the expected wedding would be at risk, and so it goes on and on.

I think the reason that an Iranian couple often separate from each other when they live overseas is their acknowledgement of the high expectations from each other. Men come to the point that they don't need to pay continuously for the affection of their wives, especially when they see how German women almost never request presents, and sometimes they even "go Dutch" and pay for themselves in a restaurant.

Iranian women on the other hand recognize that they don't need to be always at the service of their men. They can move around freely without the official permission of their husbands if they want to go abroad for a few days. They don't need to tolerate the abuse of their husband's family and their continuous interferences with their marital affairs. They realize that they don't have to stand in the kitchen every day, and thus, don't have to be concerned with what to cook or about keeping things in pristine condition.

Persian women are perpetually under the stress of being replaced by a younger woman. As the law allows temporary marriages or even a second wife, there are always a lot of competitors. This temporary marriage is called "*sigheh*," or indulgence marriage. The contracts of this kind of marriage could last from 30 minutes up to 99 years, even if men are already married. In a temporary marriage, a Shiite tradition, everything is governed in advance and by contract. Especially the dowry the amount of money that a man has to pay a woman at the wedding, referred to as the marriage dole. The marriage contract can be extended as long as desired, although the whole procedure appears to be uncomplicated, but the temporary marriage is a touchy issue.

The rules for an indulgence marriage are printed in a blue booklet, the "marriage certificate". The booklet is a charter certificate for travelling together and for sharing a hotel room. Without the "marriage certificate", extra-marital affairs can be legally punished by a hundred whiplashes, or even a stoning.

Men can enter temporary marriages with several women at the same time. Divorce is automatic at the end of the day to which the marriage has been limited in advance. For example, the contract says the couple is married from 12 pm Thursday until 8pm Sunday. Such marriage passports are being issued in registrar's offices or even in hotels. A temporary marriage, consummated at the hotel, costs about 30 Euros.

Women who agree to these short "indulgence marriages"don't have a good reputation in society, but they are often forced to do so because of poverty and solitude.

Since I had already learned as a small girl in Iran that the society and most of the families raise boys to become Pashas and girls to become servants, I always wanted to have short hair and to look like a boy, although I was an entirely delicate girl and actually proud of my gender as a girl. I wanted to be as free as my brothers who could just leave the house in the middle of the night, go for a walk or buy something at the kiosk on the corner. I'd rather be a sparrow than a snail. I didn't want to stand in the kitchen and have my mother explain the difference between parsley, basil and other herbs to me, but I wanted to sit next to my father and watch him play chess with his friends.

I didn't want to limit myself into a small world, a girl's world that was unfair in all aspects.

Millions of women in the Middle East are asking themselves every day: "Why was I born a girl?"

For Persian women, a marriage with a European partner can be ideal. They get the air to breathe and to feel the freedom they need. Persian women are usually homebodies, endearing, intelligent and flexible. They can quickly conquer the hearts of foreign men and their family. Persian men, if they thought more liberally they could probably have a successful marriage with a European woman, since they are usually family-oriented, warm, funny and generous.

When I called my husband in his office for the first time and asked him what I had to prepare for dinner, he told me that he would bring something. He brought fresh bread, cheese, olives and grapes. We set the table together and cleaned the table together thereafter. That's how easy it could be; but for me, it was a whole new world.

In my experience, German women are versatile and full of energy. They assume the mother role; they take care of education and the kids' homework and the household chores. They also work at the office. They are well-informed about what has happened in their own country and around the world. They take care of their friends and the family; they follow up on invitations and other duties. And all that will be done without complaints, nagging or demands for an extra bonus. Historically, it's not surprising that German women were instrumental in the reconstruction of the country after World War II and they were ready to join the work force powerfully. I have great respect for German women because of this.

On the other hand, I'm surprised at how little German women seem to care what they look like. Of course you look tired after a long day of work, and many of them will not bother themselves to retouch their appearances with makeup or to just powder it off. They are self-confident and also feel less pressure than Persian women who can get replaced by a younger woman easily. If you ask German women where they take the strength from, they say: "You have to go through it." They don't spend too much time worrying about things; they just act and do it.

From a historical perspective, the German women rebuilt tirelessly and with full dedication after World War II. They called *"Trümmerfrauen"* or in English "Rubble women", but sometimes they also forget the truth that they are women. They are strong and sometimes talk harshly. They might even have a little bit of a male appearance. They laugh loudly and uninhibitedly. They meddle in all matters; no matter it is economy, politics or tax issues. They don't let themselves be spoiled by their husbands or limited to their household matters.

Persian women always try to show their feminine side first by acting and speaking softly. In Iran, women have to wear pants in public after Islamic dress-code. In Germany, women don't have to do that and nevertheless, many women wear pants. I think it often makes them look a bit masculine. If Persian women had a choice of what to wear, most of them would prefer to wear skirts or dresses.

The conversation among women in the hen parties or generally in Tehran is usually about beauty matters, body figure, the latest haircut, great songs, manicures and pedicures, dresses, jewelry and the new boutiques, but sometimes about exhibitions, museums or other cultural matters. Politics is taboo for some fancy women except during the election. Persian women like to be women and they apply their charms everywhere they can to get ahead. In all Middle Eastern countries, beautiful women are admired and often preferred. Even all the suppressions and limitations placed on women, many young, proud, self-confident and intelligent women aim to lead the future of their countries.

My father and his nurse

After my beloved father had suffered a stroke, my mother was overwhelmed with work had to look for a caregiver for him. She put an advertisement in a local newspaper, which was answered by a young nurse. With my father's permission, my mother hired her.

One day, my mother asked the nurse if she could bathe my father. At first, she didn't answer at all and pretended not to have heard the question.

As the nurse had great respect for my mother, she came to me shortly after and explained very politely that, in accordance to Islamic law, my father was a stranger to her. If she had to see him naked or touch him, my father would have to marry her temporarily for the time of the caretaking, or otherwise, it wouldn't be appropriate for her to bathe him.

After she called it a day and left the house, I talked to my mother. It was a hard pill for her to swallow, and angrily she said: "I am looking for a hand, not for a second wife. " The caregiver did not return. I believe if it was up to my father, he would not have minded it. I cannot imagine what would have happened in Germany if all the caregivers, male or female, were to marry their patients in order to do their jobs.

Grocery store at night

Once, I was picked up by a taxi driver who I recongized from my previous trip. Usually the ride from the international airport to the downtown Tehran takes up to 90 minutes without traffic, but upon my arrival in Tehran at 2am I felt too hungry after a long flight to wait that long before eating. I asked the friendly taxi driver if there was a place where I could grab something to eat on my way home.

"Unfortunately not," he said and then he added, "Unless we find a grocery store on our way."

Shortly into our ride, we saw a small local store called "*dokan*" with the lights on. We stopped and entered. By then, it was about 2:30 am.

Immediately, a boy of about eight years came to the counter and asked, "What can I do for you?" as if it was an ordinary business hour that late at night!

"Are you alone here?" I asked.

"No," the child answered and added, "My father and brother are sleeping in the back, and I am helping the customers till in the morning." I was shocked and suddenly wrapped up in sorrowful thoughts for a moment.

Something like that would not happen in the West. I was choked up and tried hard to hold back my emotions.

"I would like to get something to eat." I said.

"Would you prefer something cold or warm?" The boy asked.

"Something warm if it's possible." I answered. I thought it might be a warm soup or something like that.

"OK, please wait. I have an idea. You are our guest here."

Apparently he knew that I lived abroad and I was visiting Tehran. How did he know that? I don't have a clue; my accent maybe?

A few minutes later, his older brother had woken up, switched on the lights and spread a Persian rug on the floor. Quickly, on the rug he spread a tablecloth with a Persian pattern. He then politely asked us to have a seat, brought tea and dates and told me that his father was cooking something for us. A cold shiver swept down my spine. I was really embarrassed that so many people had to make an effort to accommodate me in the middle of the night.

The father brought us a warm meal à la silhouette. It was very delicious; an omelet made with onions, tomatoes, eggs and fine spices with warmed bread. It was served with a lot of respect, love and hospitality. I wondered how they could make such an effort for a stranger in the middle of the night!

I am so glad that in Tehran there are still people who care for strangers; those who take their time to help, people who do their best to make you feel at home. Those kind people's effort in the middle of the night could never be paid with any amount of money.

Experiences like that embolden me; they give me a sense of safety, security and a feeling of belonging. I ask God to give me the opportunity to return love to these lovely people. My compatriots, May God protect you from all the bad and vicious conspiracies against you.

I have worked for UNESCO for several years, and gained much experience in different fields. I am hoping one day I would be able to set up free vocational training workshops in different parts of Tehran for those young people who could not pursue their educations because they were forced to taking care of their family in such early age.

Shoemaker

There are professions which almost do not exist anymore in our modern society, like shoemaking.

There are still Shoemakers and cobblers in Tehran who are working outdoors on the streets. These are often old men who cannot afford to own a shop; nevertheless they have to work through old age and senility. They cannot afford to retire because they have to feed their families. They sit outside even when it is cold with callous hands marked by age and red from the cold. Their sole property consists of a stool, a small stand and a side box. Often, there are two tea cups with tea spoons and a sugar bowl on the side.

One day on my way to Bazar, I went to one of the shoemakers and politely greeted him *"Salam"*, which means "Hello". I asked him to polish my boots.

He looked at me pleasantly and replied, "OK, but you have to be patient for a few minutes."

Then, with exceptional friendliness, he said, "Would you like some fresh tea with dates?"

I was touched by his generosity and charm. What he had offered me to drink and eat was almost worth more than what he charged me for polishing my boots. He was a small modest man, bent with age, and his warm heart shone through.

When I asked him, "Can I take a picture of you?" he answered with a benign smile, "Yes, but I don't want to end up on Facebook!" He was absolutely aware of everything that was going on in the modern world.

I asked myself how I could help these wonderful people.

Blind beggar

Time and time again, I had noticed a beggar who was sitting next to a restaurant trying to earn his living there. He was well-known and everyone called him "blind pauper".

One day, I took my restaurant leftovers with me, and also ordered some food exclusively for him. It was lunchtime and he was probably hungry.

I approached him and knelt on the ground in front of him. Since I knew he was blind, I took his hand, put it on the food package and the bottle of Coke which I had brought along. Coke is very popular in Iran. "Baba, here is some food and drink for you" I said.

Baba is a word used for elderly men; it's a friendly and respectful term that means "father".

He looked at me with his clouded eyes, "Mam, God may make you even more beautiful than you are." He answered and I was shocked.

He smiled at me and then added, "I can still see, but just a little bit, and nobody knows it."

I promised him that certainly not even a soul would hear it from me.

Foreigners

Foreigners are generally very popular in Iran, as are foreign products. In particular, German products have a special place and reputation as reliable, safe, durable and high quality. People from Europe or America are well-liked. For those people, Iranians use the term "foreigners", but this term unfortunately does not apply to people from the neighboring countries.

Once, when I was standing in the line at Tehran airport passport control, my eyes involuntarily zoomed on a man. He looked baffled and confused, apparently not knowing in which line he had to stand. There were two lines at passport control, one for Iranians and one for foreigners. Then someone from security addressed him loudly and asked, "Are you Iranian or a foreigner?"

He answered in a voice which sounded quite naïve, "I don't know. I have an Afghan passport." He just hadn't thought that he would fall into the "foreigners" category.

Doctors

In Iran, doctors treat their patients very attentively and with friendliness. Often they know a lot about the private lives of their patients, in addition to their diseases. They know about the patient's mother or grandmother, about whether the daughter has passed the university entry exam or if the son has found a new job. They try to build a bridge of trust and sincere rapport between them and their patients.

In case of incurable diseases such as cancer, a patient in Iran would never be confronted immediately by the doctor with the diagnosis. You would never hear him say: "You have cancer and there is no therapy for it." No. Doctors always put a lot of effort into reassuring the patient by telling everything may develop differently, and there will be always hope: "We do all we can. People are stronger than they think. Please do not panic."

When I delivered my daughter in Germany, I had to learn to my deepest sorrow that she was suffering from Down syndrome, a congenital disorder. It meant she would have to live a life with physical and mental handicaps.

I was devastated. Desperately, I asked the Doctors whether my daughter would one day be able to communicate with me. All of them answered me: "Indeed, no. They may often make loud noises. It's very unlikely that your daughter would one day be able to speak normally." The nurses also told me: "If you want to tell your kid something, you will have to repeat that a hundred times until she understands you. It is very exhausting. Prepare yourself for it."

The Doctors and nurses were very straightforward and matter-of-fact and showed very little compassion. I wish they would have treated me more thoughtfully and with more sympathy. I wish they would have encouraged and emboldened me to face the reality during the very vulnerable postpartum period of my life. I thank God that my daughter has developed her communicative abilities and many other talents despite the very sober predictions and diagnosis by the Doctors.

My daughter is 25 years old now and she speaks German better than I do. She is almost self-reliant, makes wonderful paintings, dances and sings touchingly. For almost four years, I visited a computer class with her three times a week. Thanks to that, she knows her way around social media very well. Today, through Facebook she has found many friends all around the world. With her positive attitude to the life and her delicate soul, she is our sunshine.

My girl has wonderful blue eyes. I had always wished for a daughter with the deep blue eyes.

One day, when I was visiting a morbid relative in a Tehran hospital, she asked the doctor: "Doctor, do you find my situation hopeless and incurable? Is there a slim chance?"

The doctor was aware of her malignant illness, of which she didn't have a chance to get well or heal completely. He knew she would not get back on her feet again. Nevertheless, he didn't let her notice the bitter truth, and in order to alleviate her anxiety, he replied: "In the hand of mighty God, we doctors are just very small tools. We pray and still we're hoping against hope that you would recover, because we have a gracious God that likes all of his children. Please trust in God and in us. We do our best and God will guide us."

Private practices in Tehran are magnificent. Often, the most beautiful girls work as doctor's assistants and mostly, they aren't older than 30. Rarely have I seen older doctor's assistants in doctor's offices.

Once I saw a patient come in and said to the Doctor: "Doctor, I came to your office sick, but after seeing so many beautiful girls here I feel much better now. I think I'm cured and can go home now." There are always compliments and humor even among sick people in a doctor's office.

The pretty assistants often receive gifts from the patients, mainly from the gentlemen. However, usually it is done in secrecy to prevent gossip.

Doctors usually have very friendly relation with their patients and take their time with them. One day, when I visited my brother in his private surgical office in the north of Tehran, I experienced firsthand how warmly he treated his patients. He hugged them and asked with great interest how their holidays had been, whether they were well-rested and if they had taken beautiful photos.

No one complains about waiting long for his/her turn. The waiting time passes entirely in a very friendly atmosphere with the latest news and gossips among the patients. Some even smile, laugh and tell jokes. A patient told me: "The doctor is very nice and competent. He takes care of his patients, physically and emotionally."

The behaviors of doctors in Tehran towards their patients are everything but distanced or merely superficially friendly. You can feel that their commitments really come from the heart and their patients notice that.

Bank holidays

Foreigner vistors should note that in Iran, Friday is the weekly holiday, and the week begins on Saturday. But apart from the weekly non-business day, there are other important days in the calendar. For instance, for the New Year all public offices and some stores stay closed for two weeks.

The night leading up to the last Wednesday of the year marks the celebration of *Chaharshanbe Suri*, which means "Wednesday Fire celebration" and is a part of New Year's celebrations. On this day, small fires are lit everywhere and traditionally, everyone, young and old leaps over the fire before sunset. I remember when we were kids our parents embraced us and we jumped over the fire.

People ask the fire for warmth and purification while jumping over it by saying, "My paleness shall be yours and your redness shall be mine", with "redness" standing for strength, energy, warmth and health and "paleness" symbolizes weakness, negative energies and diseases. The fire is to burn all the negative and aggravating energies by sending it up to the sky along with the smoke.

This celebration used to be very entertaining without any incidents, but unfortunately nowadays the youths often use it as a pretext to run riots. Contrary to how it used to be, there are sometimes giant fires being lit leading to accidents and injuries. The younger generation in particular celebrates this evening very boisterously. They feel free, sing, dance and laugh.

Shortly after *Chaharshanbe Suri*, there is *Nouruz*, the Persian New Year's celebration, which is also a springtime festival. It falls on the 20th or 21st of March, the exact moment of the Vernal equinox in the northern hemisphere. This celebration has a tradition spanning thousands of years.

Persians prepare for weeks in advance, including spring cleaning for their homes. They have bought pretty new clothes, because for *Norouz* ceremonies you absolutely have to wear something new from head to toe. The hustle and bustle before *Noruz* makes the face of the entire city more lively and exuberant; also the streets are overcrowded with shoppers leading up to the ceremonies.

The exact time at which the New Year begins is being calculated precisely and can fall in different hours. The actual moment of the turn of the year will change annually; sometimes it's in the evening, sometimes in the afternoon or early in the morning. The celebration begins exactly at the last second of the year.

Shortly, before the turn of the New Year, the family gets together to pray, especially for peace and a better world, but for personal wishes as well. After the change of the year they kiss each other, often a poem will be recited and then presents are exchanged. It is tradition that the older ones give gifts to the younger and the rich to the poor.

On this day, the special meal is served called *Sabzi polo* and consists of rice with herbs and fish served on the side.

Smaller children get little presents or some money for *Nouruz* from relatives. Many people use this time to visit the graves of their loved ones at the cemeteries and pray for their souls.

The last part of the festivities for New Year is *Sizdah be-dar* and it's celebrated thirteen days after New Year's Day, usually on the 1st or 2nd of April. On this day, the Persians leave their homes to enjoy an outdoor picnic. They eat, chat, play and sing. Sometimes some good pranks, ridiculous or ludicrous tricks are played on one another, as it is customary in Germany on the 1st of April.

It's a part of the tradition the seeds that have been planted usually 20 days before *Norouz* are thrown into a river symbolizing the circle of life.

Another custom is that young unmarried women will knot two blades of grass while wishing wholeheartedly and intensely for finding a husband.

Sometimes one can also see older women who are still single knotting grass and usually far away from the others' sight. They firmly believe that they will find their longed-for partners, and not even a single woman would like to miss out this opportunity and wait for the next year *Sizdah be-dar*.

Chaharshanbe Suri and *Sizdah be-dar* are purely Persian celebrations, not Arabic ones and they have been celebrated since Zoroaster's time. The same applies to *Mehrgan* celebration. This is a festival of friendship, but also a Thanksgiving festivity that is celebrated on the 8th of October. The date marks the beginning of the cold season and following traditions, people thank the Old Persian Goddess of Love and Light and ask for the harvest to be copious and abundant until springtime comes.

Finally, in summer, the so-called rain festival, *Tirgan*, is on the calendar. This holiday also dates back to ancient Persian traditions, more specifically to the angel Tir, who is said to have brought rain in a period of long-lasting drought.

Persian wedding

An entire book could be dedicated alone to the subject of Persian weddings.

Persian weddings are very interesting and dazzling events, but the road leading to them can be very complicated. In the case of weddings, Persians are particularly tradition-minded and prioritize customs that are strongly anchored and deeply rooted in Persian culture. For the bride and groom, relatives and friends, a wedding and everything related to it in advance is something special.

A wedding does not only consist of the actual marriage ceremony and the reception. Before all these take place, many issues need to be clarified to make sure the families abide by traditional customs.

Generally speaking, In Iran a marriage is not just a bond between a man and a woman; it is a connection between two families. The man not only does propose to the woman of his dreams, but he must introduce himself to the parents of his would-be bride and ask their permission and blessing for this marriage. Naturally, this happens in due form and with adequate respect. For this proposal, the man will be supported by his parents and sometimes also by his siblings. Usually, the groom's mother calls the bride's mother and asks for a formal marriage proposal introduction date. During the visit to the house of the bride's parents, pleasantries are exchanged and they talk about a possible wedding. Even if the young man and woman have already agreed on matrimony, dowry and the dedication of the rest of their lives together, these traditional formalities and protocols are absolutely necessary. The meeting also serves to have both families getting to know each other and the would-be bridegroom will bring flowers, delicious candies and similar gifts.

The official approvals by the bride and her parents are announced in a small party at the bride's parental home. During this meeting which is called *Baleboroon*, all official and traditional matters are discussed. This includes the questions regarding date and location of the subsequent festivities such as the engagement party, the marriage ceremony and the wedding reception.

One issue of great importance is the determination of the dowry, or *Mehrie*, the value of which in monetary, gold, land or property must be paid by the husband in the case of divorce. The amount is included in the marriage documents, and legally secures the woman's right to claim it in the event of divorce. In general, marriage in Iran is a very costly ritual for the groom. Many young men with limited financial budgets often face a great challenge.

The wedding ceremony and the reception are often held on a same day, but occasionally, weeks or even months pass between the two events.

In Farsi language, the official engagement is called *Aghd* and it usually takes place in the bride's paternal house. It is most common that the wedding ceremony be set up in the afternoon when a clergy is invited to the house to perform the ceremony and document the marriage.

On a large, exquisite, ornamented tablecloth spread on the floor called *"Sofreh Aghd,"* various items are placed precisely and tastefully at the ceremony: a mirror, a number of candleholders, a Koran, flowers, honey, some sugarloaves, bread, cheese, fresh herbs, rock candy, red apples, gold coins and a lot of more decorative items. These objects symbolize values such as happiness, wealth, honesty, hope, copiousness, a long life and god's blessings.

During the wedding ceremony, the bride and groom sit across from the *"Sofreh Aghd"* and the guests stand behind the couple. It is tradition that young girls and women span a white silken cloth above the heads of the bride and groom and begin to rub two sugarloaves against one another as a symbol of the sweetness of love and happiness.

After being read some verses from the Koran by the clergyman and talking about the value and vows of marriage, the cleric will ask the bride if she is ready to make the pledge and enter the bond of matrimony with the bridegroom. It's a tradition that the bride is being asked three times, without expecting her response in the first two times. It is only upon the third time, that the bride will give her "Yes" and thereby agree to the marriage. To express respect to her parents she will immediately add to her response: "with the permission of my parents and elderly". With the bridegroom, things are much easier, he will say "yes" on the first time.

After exchanging the wedding rings, the official part of the ceremony is finished by tasting honey. For this, the bride and the bridegroom dip their pinkies into a bowl of honey. Then they lick the honey from the other's finger, as a symbol of a sweet life together.

The wedding party or reception happens in the evening. At such a ceremony, 200 or more guests are common. The lavish feast usually takes place in an exclusive wedding hall and no expense is spared. The banquet will be extravagant with the tables richly adorned with flowers and decorations, covered with drinks, fruit and candies, along with live music.

Not different from Germany, the first dance belongs to the bride and groom, then the guests step on the dance floor to join them. Most of the guests dance the entire evening to celebrate and the feast atmosphere can reach a fever pitch. The sumptuous wedding meal is served late in the evening and eventually, the bride and groom cut the wedding cake.

Late at night, the party finally draws to an end. Then comes the time when the bridegroom accompanies his spouse to their matrimonial home when the bride bids her parents farewell to start a new chapter of her life.

Funerals

The loss of a loved one is a sad thing in every culture, but Iranian customs of paying last respects are even more doleful.

Although the word Mausoleum is traced back to the absolutely impressive tomb of ancient Persian King Mausa, cemeteries in Iran are rarely beautiful. They have neither decent greeneries nor any beautiful architecture or graceful statues. Altogether, they have no appeal at all. You see just dust and graves and many loud mourning people in black. There are a lot of large holes dug in the ground ready to be filled by corpse, and next to each of them are piles of dirt. Whenever I am in a graveyard, I feel a cold shiver running down my spine, and I feel frightened; I sense the need to leave immediately.

A Muslim dead body is put into the grave naked, wrapped only in a white shroud. The corpse may not be buried in a coffin, because the cadaver must be touch and be rested in the soil. Dirt and stones are poured onto the lifeless body in the grave. Experiencing such a burial is very traumatic and painful.

I was allowed to attend the funeral of my grandfather when I was a little girl. Frightened and crying, I said to my mom: "When I die, I don't want to be buried like that. I don't want my face and my body to be destroyed by such heavy tomb stones. That's not nice." And I added: "If a baby or a beautiful young girl is interred, stones will be supposed to be put on the grave, too?"

At a funeral, everyone is dressed in black. The men have beards; they are not supposed to shave when they are in mourning. They might appear slovenly at first glance, but it's a sign of sorrow, mourning and lamentation. On these occasions, and only then, women are not rouged. Some relatives sit at the grave crying for hours. It is not unusual for an immediate relative to drop her/himself on the grave and sobbingly screams: "I don't want to go on living without you!" I found it unbearable.

In Iran I cannot handle funerals emotionally. I never could. It is too sad, teary and poignant; I become emotionally overwhelmed by it.

At the funeral, a cleric will give a eulogy at the grave. Much is said about the deceased, also things that might not be true.

Sometimes they make a long speech. On one occasion, I almost started to laugh during one of these speeches, because I thought the speaker did not know what he was talking about or he had certainly taken the deceased for someone else and the eulogy had been intended for another dead person.

Muslims have to bury their dead bodies within the first day. There will be a funeral within one or two days after the death. That is why there is often little time to organize the funeral. Especially if the immediate relatives are living abroad, it is hardly possible for them to be present at the funeral.

After the ceremony, the congregation is invited for a meal by one of the closest relatives. They will meet in the house of the deceased person or of an immediate relative in a restaurant or in a room rented for the occasion. During the meal they talk about the deceased and almost burst out crying again. At the official funeral in the mosque, tea, coffee, herbal drinks and water are served along with dates and other traditional mourning sweets called *Halva*. A large and elaborate lunch or dinner is served by immediate relatives in the house after the official funeral.

I hadn't lived for a long time in Germany, when I accompanied my future husband to his uncle's funeral. It was my first experience of another kind of funeral. I couldn't believe my eyes. The mourners were dressed elegantly stylish. All the women wore light make-up, beautiful costumes and magnificent hats or black laced scarves.

There were a lot of floral wreaths carrying a big ribbon, on which the family name could be read; he was German-Austrian nobility. The uncle was to be buried on a private tomb on the mountain peak in a natural park. The path leading to the tomb was carpeted with pretty, fresh flower leaves. Everything was wonderfully in harmony with the mountain environment. The path was lined by countless old trees. On each tree there was a large wreath ornamented by a wide ribbon on which the surname of a family was written along with their coats of arms - all noble families in Europe and some from large companies such as Mercedes-Benz. It was like a dream.

The procession of mourners moved solemnly. Women dressed in beautiful costumes, elegant hats or long cloths, walked on their husbands' right sides and added to the grace and glory of the scene. The ladies wore elegant but practical shoes with low heels for walking, and carried very small purses in hands. The gentlemen wore elegant suits with a yellow rose on the lapel to match the graveside flowers.

The coffin was covered with flowers, exclusively in the colors of the house, the flag and the coat of arms. Six gentlemen in two rows lifted the coffin into the carriage. The carriage started very slowly. Up front and just behind the carriage the older mourners, walked slowly. There were many black Mercedes, also decorated with flowers and a wide ribbon in the colors of the house, black and yellow; all in an amazing harmony and homogeneity!

Behind the older guests, the younger people walked quietly and solemnly to the grave. The carriage, the limousines and the guests all moved very slowly and quietly. Only the steps on the path were heard.

The priest stood at the graveside in a very nice garment. As the coffin was being lowered into the grave, the musicians standing on the right side of the graveside started to play a march and young uniformed men standing on the left side fired cannon salutes.

At that time, the mourners were able to bid the deceased farewell once again. In front of the grave there were two terracotta vases. One was filled with yellow roses and the other with dirt and a small shovel next to it. Each mourner stepped up to the grave one by one to offer a prayer or blessing for the deceased's soul and then threw a rose into the grave and a shovel of dirt. All of it happened in silence.

When my husband and I were standing at the grave, I felt suddenly overwhelmed by emotions. I remembered the Iranian funerals, and it brought tears to my eyes. My husband noticed it immediately, took me by elbow and said very quietly, "You must control your emotions. Look at the uncle's kids how they stand at the grave upright like soldiers. They do not show their emotions in front of the others."

Afterwards, he added, "You can mourn discreetly and silently, on your own…"

After the funeral, we went into a room beautifully adorned with flowers and candles. In front of the entrance there was a table on which a large portrait of the uncle was set and next to it a candle and flowers. There was also a condolence book along with an elegant pen. Everyone could silently pay homage and last respects to the deceased, write down something nice in the memorial book and bid farewell in a private and personal manner.

A meal followed, wine and water were served. During the meal, the guests quietly talked without crying.

Literally, their logic for acceptance of death as an inevitable destiny and celebration of life profoundly moved me. It did not surprise me; Germans are very disciplined and logical.

For Muslims, the funeral service will be repeated on the third, seventh and the fortieth day as well as one year after the death of the late person. There is nothing like that in Germany. Every individual can go to the cemetery and mourn the loss of the loved ones anytime that person wishes without having to keep track of certain days.

When the funeral service of my husband's uncle drew to an end, I asked my husband, "When I die, will I be buried the same way, too?" He answered, "Yes, of course!"

In that moment, I finally let go of my fear of dying and being buried without coffin in the Persian fashion.

Banks

Banks in Iran are exactly what any customer would expect them to be. All business is processed in person and in an eye-to-eye, cordially and friendly manner.

Usually the banks are located in beautiful buildings; the entrance doors are made from massive wood and give an air of elegance. The interior and the wall coverings are usually made from the finest decorative wood. In the waiting area there is elegant and classy leather furniture that makes waiting comfortable. Everything is arranged tastefully and invitingly.

Amazingly, everywhere you look, you can see what the banks are all about: money in abundance sorted by value, color, size and bound together with a white ribbon. The money bills are piled up everywhere, tons of them on the bank director's desk and on the employees' as well, money that's worth millions.

If a customer wants to withdraw a large amount of money, the bank employee can simply draw it from the pile. The money is readily available in front of him. Due to security reasons there is a bulletproof glass screen separating customers from the staff.

Banks in Iran are often quite crowded, so you have to take a number and often wait for a while until your turn is called. Online banking is not popular yet, so people go to the branch office for each and every bank business or transaction.

The bank's employees are very helpful and friendly. Often, they will serve their customers a cup of fresh tea and dates.

As a young woman you might also receive a friendly invitation for a date along with your savings book or your bank card. It is usually written in nice words and formulated cautiously. It is not on the bank's routine service descriptions but it is complimentary.

Wishes come true

I don't know why, but as a young girl, whenever I daydreamed about marriage and having kids, I would longingly wish for son who was a blue-eyed, blonde, curly hair boy like a prince from the tales in the kids' books. Considering my Persian origin, it was actually unthinkable. But apparently some wishes do come true.

Many years later, in my second home country Germany, I got this blue-eyed blond boy. My son is already a young man; he studies psychology in Vienna, and is a wonderful, empathic, polite and very helpful person.

He lives in a house with three other students; two of them study philosophy and the third studies psychology too. I can just imagine what they discuss at the kitchen table. It probably would be too deep and philosophical for me to ever understand.

I guess I knew my son would be a philosopher or psychologist from very early on. When my son was very small, we were invited by my mother-in-law for New Year's Eve. After dinner, playing board games was planned, and my mother-in-law's 93 year-old nanny joined in. My son fetched the game, and since he had just started reading and learning math a little, he proudly announced: "We are going to play a game for everyone from 5 to 90 years! "

We started the game and had a lot of fun, until at one point nanny wanted to join the game, too. Then my son told her: "Dear nanny, unfortunately you can't play, because you are 93. "

We used to have cats and of course I had to buy cat food often. My kids liked to stack the cans into the shopping cart.

One summer day, we visited our nanny whose name was Emmi, in her small apartment. Emmi was old, she had hardly any good teeth left and due to her age, she could no longer cook for herself and often ate canned food.

My son was thirsty and he asked Emmi if he could get himself something from the fridge. Emmi said "Yes, sure" and my son went toward the fridge, when he opened the door of the refrigerator and saw many small cans in there; he quickly slammed the door and came back to Emmi.

He asked her: "Why do you eat cat food? Dear Emmi, you should cook something for yourself or order pizza. Do not take the food away from the animals. "

My son was about nine years old when he asked me one day to drive him to a friend.

In the car, I noticed a small bag which he was trying all the time to hide from me.

Out of curiosity, I asked him what he had in the bag. "Nothing" he replied shortly. I was curious and intentionally stopped at a gas station. He liked gas stations very much. While I filled the car, he wanted to take a look at the magazines and to buy a soda. It was when I seized the opportunity and looked into his bag; surprisingly I found there his new shoes.

When he came back, I asked quite carefully why he had brought his new shoes. He apologized, looked down and said: "My friend's brother very soon has got his confirmation ceremony at the church, and my friend Luca does not have suitable shoes, the family cannot afford to buy new clothes for all children. I want to give him my new shoes. "

Hugging him, I told that how much I was proud of him and his good deed.

One day, my two kids insisted on having a guinea pig. They were about six and eight years old at the time. My daughter wanted a female, my son a male guinea pig. In order to prevent their guinea pigs from mating all the time, we had finally decided to buy two male animals.

My son immediately noticed it, but my daughter did not, therefore she named her guinea pig "Anastasia" and my son gave his guinea pig his own Christened name "Philipp".

After a few months, they were both sitting in front of the guinea pigs' cage and my daughter nagged her brother, "Why don't they make children?"

My son said quite calmly, "They can't have kids, because they are gay. "

Most probably, he had picked up this word at school at his age.

One summer, a girlfriend of mine took me and my little children along to Spain. One day, we went to see a bullfight; I had never been to such an event and had no idea how cruel it could be.

Shortly after the bullfight began, I felt that I had no guts and was not able to see such a brutality. My two kids were sitting next to each other with furious faces, because they do love all animals. Once, someone had told my son that his dog was ugly, he had sadly replied: "Animals cannot be ugly. "

We left the arena and waited in the coffee shop for the others. My kids didn't know that the bull was killed at the end of the fight; it was formidable and hideous enough as it was up to that point.

At that moment, my friend anxiously showed up and asked me if I could drive back to the hotel on my own with the kids. Her husband was one of the sponsors and had financed the training of one of the Toreros who was severely injured. They wanted to go to the hospital to check on his condition.

My daughter looked at her and said: „Please, take me along, I am also worried about the bull, it was hurt badly and was bleeding. "

And my son said: "Injuring animals is neither a game nor a sport! "

Such a wise word from a little kid!

Children

In Iran, children are around and involved in all family matters, in good and bad times, regardless of their age. This gives them a sense of family bonding and a feeling of connection to each other. Above all, they gather precious experiences from an early age regarding the realities of life.

In working class families, sometimes an eight-year-old child knows more about life and his way around many situations than a fourteen year-old teenager in Germany. It is not unusual to see a ten-year-old kid running the family business in the absence of his father.

On the other hand, in wealthier Persian families, parents are usually lenient towards their children and seldomly show restrictive measures or discipline. Undoubtedly, most of the children who have been raised this way will turn out to be spoiled and self-centered, and will face various difficulties in their lives.

In Iran, there are a lot of parents who selflessly dedicate and devote themselves entirely to the raising of their children.

In family matters, kids are fully allowed to participate and to hear what's being talked about around the table, even regarding unpleasant and sad events. Persians believe there are moments of happiness and sadness in life, and by engaging children from early on in, they will gain useful experiences that can help them grow strong in facing the ups and downs of life. Sometimes they forget that children need to be children enjoying their childhood, and that they need to spare from certain unpleasant thoughts.

Iranian children often care for their parents remarkably well over the course of their lives. They do their best to make them happy and proud. I admire this quality in Persian children who are aware of the hardship and the sacrifices that their parents went through to raise them with so much love in their lives. Children feel obligated to return this love with filial affection and piety when their parents age. They truly believe the path of love is reciprocal.

One of my sisters-in-law lives in Tehran and her mother lives in Sweden. Whenever her mother has to go to the hospital, she flies there, stays at the hospital and makes her utmost effort to take good care of her.

She emphatically says, "When you're old, you need a hand to hold, you need love and warmth."

A few years ago, the Iranian film "The Separation of Nader from Simin" received Oscar award for the best foreign language movie (original title, "*Jodai-ye Nader az Simin*", 2011), dealing exactly with this issue. The movie is about a young husband who doesn't want to forego his old and sick father suffering from Alzheimer disease by living abroad with his wife in comfort. He wants to keep his father by his side and take care of him under any circumstances and by all means. One of the most impressive dialogues in the movie was the scene that the husband responded to his wife's question, "Do you really want to give up everything for the person who doesn't even recognize you?" "But I do recognize him," he replied.

When my kids were still little, my German sister-in-law often visited us. She used to whisper negative things about my parenthood into my husband's ear. She tried to make fun of what I had learned from my mom and grandma, who believed kids are the most precious treasure in a mother's life.

My sister-in-law was the know-it-all of their family. Early in the evening, she would insist that I brought my kids into their rooms, switch off the light and say "good night". I had to leave them alone, even if they were crying and could not fall asleep. Still I can hear their screams in my ears. I feel bad and still have a guilty conscience about it. Meanwhile, I had to sit in the living room listening to their boring conversations about the weather, travels, winter sales or new tax laws, and precisely follow the conversation even though I didn't want to. They kept emphasizing the point that I was living in a new world with new rules and traditions; so, I had no choice except accepting, tolerating and obeying this customs.

How can a baby feel comfortable being alone in a room shortly after birth? For nine months it has been growing in the mother's womb, and suddenly from one day to the next, it has to be all alone by itself in a room. Unfortunately, this often continues the same way till the babies become small kids. They are still supposed to go to bed early, the time when the father comes home, without question.

"Kiss, Kiss!! Off to bed! Lights off and sleep! "

"But daddy, I wanted to...! "

"We will talk about it on the weekend. "

But it doesn't change on the weekends. Unfortunately it is common in Germany that children have less contact with their fathers than with their mothers. And you can often hear, "parents need time for themselves". But I wonder, what is more important than children?

In many cases, children from affluent and well-off families are sent to a boarding school very early on. Sometimes, their parents are even traveling when children want to come home for their breaks or holidays. And then, parents complain about being left alone in their old age, when they step into senility. They complain about being rarely visited by their children or even being quartered in a retirement home. Tit for tat!

In Germany, particularly when fathers and sons are talking, I often hear, "You should never do that!"

On the contrary to that, in such conversations in Iran you would hear often, "Who would be better suited than you? Of course you can do that. You are a winner." That strengthens the self-confidence of the kids.

Parents in Germany often do not know who their children's friends are, especially when they hit teenage years.

My mother always knew everything about us, even when we were not teenagers anymore. She knew those who were around us, who we were mingling with, who were not right persons for us. She knew those friends who did not have a goal or aspiration in their lives. She knew who had problem with alcohol or smoking or who behaved badly. It was inconceivable and beyond our imagination to be in contact with our peers and classmates who had made my Mom's list of having any of those bad habits. My mom had seven children and she was never stopped trying to protect us. She took every inconvenience and annoyance on herself to keep us away from negative and destructive surroundings. She was tireless in this endeavor.

In my circle of friends, I often noticed that the children, adolescents or young adults often returned home at midnight or even in the first morning hours. When I asked my friends if they were not worried about it, I usually received the careless, and to my view, irresponsible answer: "They are over eighteen. "

I was confused. Again, I found myself caught between two cultures and ideological differences, two cultures that dealt so differently with raising, training and educating children. I didn't know what style of raising kids had better outcome.

I'm wondering why parents can't tell their children, "We shoulder responsibility for you. You are in our custody and you live with us. Besides, this house has rules that apply to you too, and one of those is the proper time of curfew at night. You cannot return home late at night. We have to know who you are friends with."

Surely, when children come of age, they will be able to decide when and where to go, and with whom to associate. Until then, I believe that the rules and regulations of the house must be obeyed. My paramount wish for my son is his happiness and I make my ultimate effort to protect him from all threats, just the same as it was in my home country, regardless of the age.

Of course it is not easy and it can be really uncomfortable, especially when a single parent is responsible.

I worried and still worry about young people who are inexperienced and have no close contacts with their parents.

As a young girl, I would never have been able to leave my home country to start a new life alone overseas, on a continent foreign to me with a diametrically different culture opposed to my own, with distinct and diverse manners, with new rules and laws, with entirely different people, if I haven't had inner strength and healthy self-confidence as the result of my upbringing.

Scheherazade

There are childhood stories in the life of every person that inspire them throughout their lives. In my case it was story of Scheherazade (Persian, *Schahrzad*). She has inspired me ever since I was a child.

Time and time again, when I meet the alternative practitioners and doctors during lectures and seminars on medicine and natural healing methods, I take the opportunity to share short stories and anecdotes about my travels or daily life. Fortunately, my tales have been well received and during lunch and dinner I am always asked by friends and colleagues to sit at their table to share some of my short stories. Sometimes I am booked to two or three tables around. They love my short stories and anecdotes.

By now, I have been given the nickname *"Schahrzad"* (the character in 1001 nights) which makes me very happy. I am truly fascinated by these stories and when I read the 1001 Nights stories every once in a while, I dive deeply and get lost in the world of fairy tales so much so that I see *Schahrzad* in my mind and can visualize her for hours – *Schahrzad*; an intriguing, happy princess with a wonderful imagination.

My discovery of knowing how to tell a story is a story in itself, and it is traced back to the time when I had to look after my siblings at the age of about seven or eight years old to keep them entertained. I was a creative kid; therefore, I came up with the idea of making up and telling tales. My mom was a school principal and teacher; she had seven kids and only little time for us due to her job.

We were five kids, my identical twin brothers came later. I was seven or eight years old when my mom passed the responsibility for all my siblings to me, although she always had a young married couple as helpers at home. She emphasized the point that I was a big girl at that age and I could easily carry the responsibilities. I had no other choice, and reluctantly took the reins of the home and my new role as a small, young mummy.

I was the first daughter and the second child; almost all of us were born with an age difference of one to two years apart.

My mother comes from a very educated family. Her grandfather was a well-known public prosecutor and later the governor of a north-eastern province, and his father had been a philosopher and a lecturer at the university, and also an honorable judge. She couldn't stay at home all the time being a housewife and so she appointed me as her substitute, a younger mummy who was supposed to take care of all siblings: feed the kids, help the children with their homework and keep them entertained.

Back then, there were only a few games available for kids, there were no other kid's programs or kids' movies other than some cartoons. I had to make things up on the spot to entertain them. As a little girl, I enjoyed making up stories.

Mostly, I told my tales in the evenings because we were afraid of the dark and I wanted to keep my siblings distracted. My mother had become a parent at the age of 16, so she desired to catch up and make up for lost time in her neglected education. She was studying at the university in the evenings after her work. We were home alone in the evenings with the couple who were busy with the household chores or otherwise they isolated themselves in their room. This is how I started: I put a small stool behind the TV (*our TV was in a locked wood-cabine*t), stood on the stool and started my tales, most of the time, without any preparation, the improvising ideas came to my mind spontaneously. Still I have no idea how I was able to devise those stories.

During the entire time of my recital, there was absolute silence. Before the kickoff, my siblings went to toilet; they knew otherwise they would miss something. It was a live performance and there wouldn't be any repetition.

My siblings were completely fascinated with my tales. They would do everything I asked them to do in order to hear them: finish their homework on time, stop cursing when arguing, or even give me some of their pocket money. I was collecting money for Mother's Day all year round.

My stories grew into series and my siblings always had to wait until the next evening for the next episode. Sometimes, they could not wait that long and would come to me to beg me to hear a bit more of the story. They were curious and excited, and so was I, because I didn't know either how the story would go on or how it would end. I had to make it up first.

At school, I couldn't really concentrate on my lessons. My mind was turning all the time around my story and how it would continue. Once, we had to write an essay about our weekend experiences. That weekend I had no time to write an essay because we had guests, and as the first girl, I had to care for setting the table, starting short conversations with the guests, serving food and so on.

Unfortunately, it was me among all the other students in the class who had to come to the blackboard to share my memories of the weekend. I was shocked, but I didn't let anyone notice my fear. I took a small, blank notebook which I had bought the very weekend and went to the blackboard. I opened my notebook and started to read from the empty notebook. Everyone liked my memories. The teacher and some of my classmates even applauded me. Suddenly, the teacher got up and angrily said: "Are you really reading from your notebook? You read a long story from such a small notebook and turned the page only once. "

Then she herself gave the answer: "I know why. You lied. You read that story offhand and not from your notebook. "

She walked up to me madly, took my notebook and showed to the pupils: "Look here, her notebook is empty! "

I was so ashamed and awfully terrified. I wished the ground would have opened up and swallowed me, I almost collapsed. I was such a proud girl and that incident wore me down for weeks.

For the entire 15 minutes recess, I had to stand in front of the mean class captain holding a heavy book on my head with a leg up at the same time, a humiliation that has lingered in me for years.

I had obviously been overstrained, really overburdened with both my homework and my siblings. I had frequently heard: "it is the act that counts". To my view, I had read my essay, my way or the other way, it didn't matter, either way. I was only nine years old at that time. When I complained to my mom about the teacher in the evening, she told me: "You aren't supposed to go to school without your homework and I will have to go to school tomorrow to apologize to the teacher for your cheating."

My motherly duties were more important to me than my school assignment. I continued to care for my siblings, I checked every day if their homework was done, if everything was correct and properly written, if their school bags were clean, if all pencils were pointed and sharpened, if the uniforms were ironed, everything, actually, and I had to think about my tales too.

My stories were about Kings and Queens, Princesses and Princes, about Heroes and Witches, about happiness and grief, victory, loss, and about family... Unfortunately back then, nobody came to the idea to write down my tales otherwise who knows, maybe my stories could have become as popular as "Harry Potter's"? I've forgotten them all now.

After a while, my stories became increasingly popular and gradually well-known through word of mouth. When it was tale-time, we had visitors from the neighborhood and our circles of friends and relatives, particularly on the weekends.

At the weekends, my stories were longer. When I narrated, I drew the curtains to allow only a little light in, in order to create a movie theater atmosphere and especially because I had to change my voice all the time, I didn't want my audience to watch me doing that.

I was a princess for a moment and a prince the next; once bad, once good, the protagonist and antagonist was just me, the entire castdom, the music, and the onomatopoeia; I was wind and thunder, I was shots and cries, I was wolf and lion, and I was witch and angel.

It sounded really authentic; sometimes the children got frightened and hugged each other during my narratives. Sometimes I got scared myself, but I was the oldest and had to be brave. My older brother never attended my performances, he didn't like me.

Sometimes my little audience shed happy tears over a happy ending and they clung to me thankfully and happily. The kids loved me and they were willing to do everything to show me their gratitude. I felt a power in me and asked them not to call me Susan or sister anymore but Aziz, that means "precious" or "dear"; a name I love to this day.

My father had given me his full support and authorization, and my mother called me her right hand. For these meaningless terms and metaphors I was under stress from morning to evening, from dawn to dusk and I had to forget that I was a child myself. Sometimes, it was all too much for me, some evenings I could hardly sleep, but I wanted to make my listeners happy with my fairy tales and performances.

In elementary school, I was not a good student; I hardly had free time to study or do my homework and little concentration. Later, I developed an idea: performing my fairy tale and staging little stories with my audience on special occasions for birthdays, the summer party or for the New Year.

We lived in a large house with a large basement in which we had lots of clothes and pieces of furniture. We also had a lot of wigs. My mother owned various wigs; it was fashion then.

On the first occasion, I wrote the invitations for the summer party myself. After dinner, I led the guests into the room set up for the show. In the meantime, I had put all my cast into costumes and told them what they had to do and say. Sometimes, we had rehearsal for days. We had a big curtain hung up in the room and my performers were behind the stage waiting for my orders. With the help of the neighbors, we provided folding chairs for the audience.

At first, I appeared as the moderator on the stage. After a greeting and welcome, I talked like a pro about the program. I went behind the stage, changed my costume, and came back on the stage.

We recited poems, sang, danced in Persian, Indian, Turkish and Arabic style, and staged a short story. The audience was amused and entertained; they thanked us and then moved on. It is a pity that nobody took a picture or wrote something down about it, nobody thought about my artistic soul. Alas! For them, my performance was merely entertainment, but for me it meant a lot of effort and many sleepless nights.

Persians usually suffer from doctor-mania. Almost all parents wish their kids to become doctors, no matter what they're interested in, talented or gifted.

One day, siting in the living room, my mother asked me in the presence of a few guests what I wanted to become later when I grow up and what my favorite profession was. Immediately I answered: "Actress", because I was already an actress, after all.

She got up and with a heavy hand slapped my face, and then adamantly said: "Never say that again, understand? Never ever! "

Still, I can feel the weight of her hand on my face and I'm suffering from that to this day, because I know I could become a good actress or singer, and her slap still hurts me. Why are some parents so insensitive? For my performances, they applauded me, but they prevented me from following my dream, my flair, my capability and my path; a path I had talent for.

The Mother's Day that I organized was another painstaking but popular event at our home. I collected money for my mother all year long. Every night before children went to bed I asked them for money, like a tax collector. They had to give me one percent of their allowance every night. No exceptions.

Sometimes they didn't have money, in that case a small interest would be added to the regular amount and they were allowed to pay me the next day. Sometimes when they were too stressed out about it and were crying, my father got involved and paid off their debts. It was strenuous and exhausting for me to levy the money every evening, but after a year and with the help of my dad who accompanied us shopping, we could treat my mother to a big surprise.

I lined up my siblings who were all dressed up nicely, everyone had to recite a short essay for mommy and give her a present. That created a very good atmosphere with a lot of love and warmth. We always had spectators from the family for that ceremony and we kept on doing this until we became teenagers.

Shahrzad

One day, the ruler of Persia caught his wife in the act with a slave. He was so bitter about it that he decided to take a cruel revenge: he married women and let them get killed the next day.

Therefore, the families of young women lived in great fear. For the mighty caliph chose another woman every day and kept them in his palace, to have them killed the next morning.

This was also what happened to Shahrzad's best friend Shiva. This was exactly the reason why Shahrzad had volunteered - for she wanted to take revenge against the mighty ruler. But then, it all came unexpectedly different....

On the first evening, Shahrzad told him a nice story and the caliph was mesmerized by Shahrzad's charms and her wisdom. He wanted to hear more stories. Shahrzad promised him to tell a new fairy tale every evening, but she said she would need the whole day to make up these tales. He agreed and that's what the famous stories of 1001 nights derived from.

The good idea: the caliph fell in love with Shahrzad, they had three children and the two lived happily ever after to the end of their lives.

Language school

I remember vividly the days when I started to learn German many years ago in Germany. I went to language school full of enthusiasm and zeal for my new life. I signed up, paid the tuition, received my books and entered the classroom highly motivated.

I kicked off with a great confidence and full concentration, but I hardly understood anything on the first day. Everything seemed strange to me, unfamiliar and difficult, and the words didn't enter my memory. I went home hopeless and helpless. The following days were just as sad and discouraging as the first day. I was feeling dumb.

German language has a very complicated grammar which makes it difficult for foreigner to learn, unless you had emigrated there at young age. For us new students the effort to build one single sentence was a most exhausting challenge. We asked our teacher how long it would take us to have a command on the German language to at least communicate properly with people in German society. The answer we got was disappointing: "At least three to five years. "

Apart from me, there were a few other young women from Iran at school. When we heard that disappointing answer, we cried. We all wanted to be able to understand German as quickly as possible, and to be understood as well. We wanted to get to know people and feel our host country. We wanted to be able to open up dialogue with the people around us. Really, did we have to wait three to five years for that?

When could we finally read the newspaper well enough to understand the local and world news? When didn't we need to embarrass ourselves anymore by using a wrong verb or article?

Our German teacher had a very serious and bureaucratic personality. He insisted first of all on learning the entire grammar correctly: Subjunctive 1 and Subjunctive 2, active and passive, direct and indirect speech. Secondly, on learning what dative and genitive were.... Hallelujah! It was all too much for us.

We were gasping for just a few words, short sentences that could help and enable us to go about our daily life; something like "Good morning", "Goodbye", "Thank you", "How do I get here or there?"... Instead, we had to start with the articles.

Dear Germans: in my homeland Iran, the sun is shining without an article, it is not masculine, feminine or neutral, it is just sun. In Farsi the articles do not exist.

I always felt uncomfortable being asked the same annoying questions every day: what country I was from and what I was doing and for how long did I intend to stay in Germany? Once, to spare myself the further unpleasant questions about my country of origin, I answered instantly and imprudently, I was from Spain. To my surprise, the lady who had asked me suddenly said something in Spanish which of course, I couldn't understand. It was very embarrassing to me; I swore I would never ever renounce my homeland again.

At the beginning, it is hard when you cannot express yourself or open up a conversation. You also can't complain about or defend yourself against anything. You end up having to accept everything. You are afraid to embarrass yourself or to make yourself ridiculous by speaking poor German with many mistakes and errors and inappropriate grammar such as dative, accusative or genitive.

In such situations, you'd rather forfeit your rights because you can't form your thoughts in German in time. And by the time you find the right articles and the correct sentence structure, your addressee might have already disappeared.

In any case, the annoying and prohibitory articles and the verbs in German language and the way you often have to split up them in different places in a sentence, should not prevent you from learning the language.

Out of this language barrier, a tendency to be more guarded and reserved might develop.

When I was first learning German, I wanted so much to understand the news, particularly the news about Iran. Since a war was broken out between Iran and Iraq, I was worried about my loved ones and my friends and I wanted to hear about my homeland.

In some countries, people do not care so much whether or not you can express yourself correctly. Often one word is enough to make people understand what you mean – and that makes you more encouraged and more motivated to talk. However, the Germans do not have that kind of patience. They lose their temper in these situations and they do not find it funny if you can't articulate what you want to say. Just God knows how often I heard these expressions: "Excuse me? ", "Say that again! ", "I can't understand you. " My girlfriends and I knew exactly how the Germans would have responded if we wanted to start communicating with them in that level of knowledge of language at that time. We got used to hearing those sentences over and over again.

We were a few girlfriends in school. After a while, we thought about leaving Germany because of its difficult language and the cold climate, but where to and how? There was a cold war between Iran and the western countries at that time, particularly with the United States. We weren't welcome anywhere and we had to be thankful for being allowed to stay in Germany. To us, this seemed unfair: what did the war between governments have to do with us? We were young women with confidence and aspiration for the future.

Two of my girlfriends from that language school now work as doctors and another one owns a very nice Persian restaurant with a small hotel.

I truly believe that in order to facilitate language learning and engage the life of immigrants, language schools should start with colorful and illustrated books, with the simple, easy sentences and short stories. They should come up with different games to make learning a foreign language more entertaining and fun. I am happy to see that nowadays in Germany such stimulating and motivating method of learning are being offered.

But one thing which was as important back then as it is today was the understanding and the support received from countless, nice, friendly and open-minded Germans.

Solitude

Often, immigrants feel pressure to view their new country as paradise or Utopia and to show gratitude always for being allowed to live there. In reality, immigrants have left their homes, in some cases were forced to relinquish their familiar surroundings, family, friends, classmates, possessions, culture, culinary habits, climate, love and warmth and the feeling of being belonging.

I am talking about the terrible cases of forced flight, caused by political and economic uncertainty, violence, wars and massacres, or by hopelessness and poverty. This causes so many pitiable people to look for shelter and fight for sheer survival. For these plagued people, Europe is a refuge in the truest sense of the word, where thankfully still every possible aid is being offered. This shield of protection helps many innocent children and defenseless oppressed people, from poor refugees to ordinary immigrants.

At home; you will always find a shoulder, a hand, a smile, even in difficult life situations. Once you leave your home country, all those disappear. As an immigrant, the only thing that matters is to remind yourself: "I have to go on. "

Giving up your beloved home is the price to be paid for a new beginning in a foreign country. It is a tedious and herculean task to start from zero. And still sometimes there is no other avenue than letting it all go, and leaving behind everything that was once dear to you.

When you're young, it is easier, but for elderly people it is often very difficult to start all over again, to learn a new language, to adapt to a new mentality and life style. In a foreign country immigrants often have to give up a part of their independence and self-esteem. As time goes by they may be filled with melancholy and depression. As they have lost their familiar surroundings and their friends, older immigrants might just lack the power and energy to cope with everything that's new. They aren't young anymore, after all.

The new language, the style of communication, the speed of changes, the administrative processes, the social, legal, cultural issues, another mentality, the whole environment and the entire surroundings, all must be processed and accepted anew.

Actually, my father never wanted to leave Iran. He was successful in his profession; he was headed towards retirement and wanted to spend the last good years in peace and comfort in his country, in which he had his friends, his hobbies, his beloved garden and everything else. But he gave in to the desire of his family and at some point reluctantly followed the others to America. The family had made the decision.

When I visited him, he was sitting in an armchair with a remote control in his hand.

I asked: "Daddy, how are you? "

With a vacant look that showed the sadness in his eyes and a muffled voice, he said: "I cannot leave the house; cannot talk to people because I don't know the language; I cannot drive because I don't have an American driver's license, I can't even go to the doctor on my own or go shopping. I only have the choice between countless TV channels; morning to evenings when the others are at work. I miss my life in Tehran! "

In the USA, he was always dependent on others. He plunged into depression; he was dramatically homesick and nostalgic until he became fatally overwhelmed with illness. It wasn't easy for him to travel to Tehran. Due to sanctions, there were no direct flights and it was very arduous for him to travel in his old age. Regrettably, he succumbed to his illness and passed away in America and was buried there, not in his homeland Iran.

Iranians neither like to be alone nor live alone. They live with their families, even if, like all families, they don't get along. Nevertheless, almost every weekend, Iranians organize reunions and look forward to spending their some quality time with their family.

When a couple divorces, it usually doesn't take long until new partners are found. Men especially won't stay alone very long. If a married couple separates, there is always a ray of hope that the elderly mediators will help them reconcile, especially if the couple has children. I appreciate this intervention, when the specter of divorce lurks. In Iran, a divorce wouldn't proceed as cold and emotionless by the lawyers and the courts as in Germany, where no relative takes even a slightest effort to ameliorate and improve the situation. The reason for that indifference is usually the cold statement that the couple's privacy must be respected.

Contrary to that, a separate couple will be not alone in Iran. Virtually, everyone attempts to mend the wounds in the hearts of a couple, to solve problems between them, and when there is no longer a chance for reconciliation, they go on the hunt for a new partner.

In Iran, family, kin and relatives, friends and acquaintances as well as neighbors act in a way that is not common in Germany. Generally, young women who wear no wedding ring will be approached at any family events and parties or in the Bazar, in a park or even in a public transportation, in a word, everywhere.

Sometimes, simply bringing two single people together for a date would lead to a marriage.

When I tell people around me in Germany that every now and then I feel lonely, they don't understand me and ask me: "Why? You've got your family. You are not alone." Yes, I have my family. But you can feel lonely although you are not alone.

Flight from Tehran

Shortly before my trip to Tehran, a Persian acquaintance that I knew well had heard about my travel plan and called me. Straightforwardly, he asked me whether I could bring him an orange tree from Iran, a tree with such great fruits as he knew from home, the one which he simply couldn't find in Germany.

I asked him how I could do that.

"Easily", he answered: "you just wrap the tree in a cling film, pour enough water and place it in its case, then put it in your suitcase. You know, the tree has to go into the suitcase otherwise you'll get into trouble at customs. After all, it's prohibited. "

"Oh, I see, but what will happen to my clothes if the water flows out? What if I get into trouble at customs?" I thought. Besides, if you put a tree in your suitcase, you'll barely have space for anything else. I thought it was crazy what people expect. Of course, I ended up not doing it.

I had almost forgotten that episode when I got on board for the return flight from Tehran to Germany on an Iranian airline. I buckled up the seatbelt and waited for takeoff.

I took a look around and I couldn't believe what I saw: across the aisle a man was sitting, and in the seat next to him a large pot was buckled, in which there was an orange tree.

When the owner of the orange tree noticed the question mark along with an exclamation on my face, he explained to me: "You know, you can't get this kind of orange tree in Germany, so..."

I was thinking what he probably meant by so…, and that who had given him permission to endanger the passengers' lives with such a large pot of dirt? What if something would happen? There are always turbulences in 10,000 feet high over Eastern Europe. I was angry and worried about it until we finally landed.

If you have good contacts and relations in Iran, unfortunately, everything is possible.

Return to Germany

After spending more than two weeks in Tehran, I am returning to Germany, to Frankfurt, a beautiful and admirable city that I missed so much.

As I arrive in Frankfurt, it rains. Everything I see is just clouds; grey on grey that causes me to feel deeply depressed and makes my return trip even more difficult. Mysteriously, it always rains when I return to Germany.

The first days after returning, I always feel melancholic and lonely. I feel a pain; a poignant pain in my heart that hurts me badly, because I don't have my family and friends around me anymore. I miss Persia's daily sun and many other things. I feel Tehran compellingly calling me back.

But then my feeling to my second home prevails upon me and fills the gap in my heart. A home that has given me so much in my life: family, security, comfort and most of all peace. In Germany, I had and still have all the opportunities to go far as a woman. My new home in which my beloved children have grown up, and are planning their own future now, where many people from all over the world of different ethnicities, mentalities and religions are living together and committed to a better and more peaceful world.

I have been blessed with two wonderful home countries, one in the East and the other in the West, with equally magnificent history and dazzling cultures which have enriched my life in so many ways and for that from the bottom of my heart, I am thankful to God.

But in my heart and soul, my beloved Persia will forever have a special place, and give me a little more sense of home.

King's Garden Bagheshah, Tehran

Mausoleum of King Kourosh

The natural and cultural diversity of Iran – large deserts.

Ancient cultural sites

Ancient Mosques.

192

Epic monuments

Experience stunning natural moments.

The author

Her roots are in Persia. There, Susan Reuss completed her political science studies, learning a lot about perspectives and their implications on life and co-existence.

Her curiosity to look behind the scenes, and her understanding of interdependencies and backgrounds led her into the editorial offices of a large, respected daily paper, where she began working as a journalist.

In 1985, her path led her to Germany, where she quickly gained a foothold, setting up her own business. Pursuant to her interest in alternative healing methods, she completed advanced training to become a certified alternative practitioner. Susan Princess Reuss practiced her profession in her own offices in Germany from 1994. Combining her expertise as both a medically certified nutritionist and as a qualified cosmetologist, she works today as a skilled consultant in the entire field of beauty, health and lifestyle.

Being the mother of a child with special needs, she feels compelled to put her skills and her international contacts to good use in service and philanthropy. She is committed to many child-care projects in Germany and abroad and was named a UNESCO attaché in 2000.

Her hobbies are creative writing, singing and photography.